THE PRICE WATERHOUSE
GUIDE TO
FINANCIAL MANAGEMENT

THE WILEY/NATIONAL ASSOCIATION OF ACCOUNTANTS PROFESSIONAL BOOK SERIES

Jack Fox • *Starting and Building Your Own Accounting Business*

Denis W. Day • *How to Cut Business Travel Costs*

Gerald M. Ward and Jonathan D. Harris • *Managing Computer Risk: A Guide for the Policymaker*

Harry L. Brown • *Design and Maintenance of Accounting Manuals*

Gordon V. Smith • *Corporate Valuation: A Business and Professional Guide*

Harvey L. Shuster • *The Financial Manager's Guide to Microsoftware*

Henry Labus • *Successfully Managing Your Accounting Career*

Ralph G. Loretta • *The Price Waterhouse Guide to Financial Management: Tools for Improving Performance*

THE PRICE WATERHOUSE GUIDE TO GUIDE TO FINANCIAL MANAGEMENT

TOOLS FOR IMPROVING PERFORMANCE

RALPH G. LORETTA

WILEY

JOHN WILEY & SONS

New York • Chichester • Brisbane • Toronto • Singapore

ISBN 0-471-62044-0

Printed in the United States of America

10 9 8 7 6 5 4 3 2 1

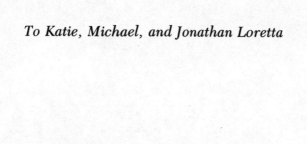

To Katie, Michael, and Jonathan Loretta

PREFACE

Today's corporate executives, eager to gain a competitive edge, expect their financial organization to apply their expertise and resources to business decision making. Although CEOs still require a sound control and reporting framework, financial organizations can no longer limit their activities to accumulating, recording, and reporting financial information. Consequently, chief financial officers and controllers face the challenge of simultaneously maintaining the independence necessary to ensure accurate and reliable financial information while contributing directly to business decision making. To successfully face these dual challenges, chief financial officers and controllers need to ensure that their financial organizations can respond effectively to management's changing needs and expectations. The practical performance evaluation techniques described in this book can help chief financial officers and controllers bring their services in line with these expectations.

To assist chief financial officers and controllers in measuring and evaluating performance, this book defines standard financial activities, identifies key areas for evaluation, and outlines an approach to conducting a structured assessment. The methodology for conducting an assessment provides a focused review at two levels. At one level, specific financial responsibilities and activities are examined using service attribute checklists. The assessment defines the structure and features within the scope of the financial services. Using performance indicator checklists, CFOs and controllers can then quantify financial services as a basis for evaluating the effectiveness of those activities to the organization.

At a second level, the methodology directs attention to the control framework of the organization comprising the policies, organizational structure, and procedures that define the overall organization, as well as the controllership function. The control framework should permit the CFO to execute effective services and support a company's essential activities. Evaluating a control framework enables the CFO to detect flaws and improve the delivery of financial services.

The financial functions discussed in this book may not apply to all organizations. Chief financial officers and controllers should use judgment in deciding which functions and evaluation techniques apply to their organization.

RALPH G. LORETTA

Cleveland, Ohio
November 1989

ACKNOWLEDGMENTS

Certain material in this book has appeared previously in publications of Price Waterhouse and is used with the permission of my partners. Acknowledgments are due many of my associates for their generous help.

My first thanks to Daniel P. Keegan, whose own outstanding work in the field inspired and served to validate many of the concepts expressed in this work. Dan not only motivated me to begin writing, but offered sustained support.

I also owe particular acknowledgment to the practitioners in the firm who helped develop the material. The contributions and collegiality of Randy Runk, Len Lindegren, and Mark Lutchen made this very much a shared effort.

Special acknowledgments should also go to Mary Ann Paul, who tirelessly assembled the material from a variety of sources and scraps of paper, and to Jeanine LeMar, who miraculously turned it into a typed manuscript.

R.G.L.

CONTENTS

CONTENTS

CONTENTS

CONTENTS

THE PRICE WATERHOUSE
GUIDE TO
FINANCIAL MANAGEMENT

1

FINANCIAL EFFECTIVENESS OVERVIEW

Companies today respond to increasing competitive pressures by reviewing their strategies and organizational structures and dramatically realigning business operations. These companies apply their creative potential to leverage strengths and correct limitations. To gain competitive advantage, they may regroup business segments to create stronger, focused units. Management at all levels demands accurate, integrated financial and operating reporting, as well as specialized decision support services.

CHALLENGES TO FINANCIAL ORGANIZATIONS

New strategies and organizations present challenges to financial organizations. Businesses that implement strategy effectively focus resources on essential services and information supporting strategy execution. As a provider of these services and information, effective financial organizations must determine the impacts and respond to the needs of these realigned organizations. Effective financial organizations focus on areas impacting the viability, growth, and success of the business to determine whether:

- Financial services required to support essential business activities are provided and meet required performance standards
- Other nondiscretionary financial services are provided and meet performance standards
- Unnecessary or redundant financial services can be eliminated

CHARACTERISTICS OF EFFECTIVE FINANCIAL ORGANIZATIONS

Financial organizations respond to management needs for essential services and information by understanding three dimensions of the business—strategy, organizational structure, and essential business activities. These dimensions shape effective financial organizations and provide a basis for evaluating the relevance, effectiveness, and productivity of specific financial services.

Effective financial organizations understand the business strategy of their organizations. Successful businesses grow by defining their goals clearly and achieving business objectives consistent with corporate philosophy and culture. Understanding strategy enables financial management to broadly define activities and functions most important for business success.

Effective financial organizations also understand the current organizational structure of the business. A formal organizational

4

structure defines entities and their reporting relationships. Organizational structures range from centralized or decentralized, to a combination of both. Regardless of approach, the financial organizational structure should map consistently with the overall organization. If operating units are highly decentralized, effective financial organizations will deploy services and resources to meet the needs of a decentralized environment. Understanding the overall organizational structure also enables the financial organization to map out information needs and determine financial service expectations throughout the company.

Understanding essential business activities is the keystone to successfully meeting the organization's information and financial service needs. Because all organizations operate within budget and resource limits, effective financial organizations will focus on supporting the limited, but essential, business activities that must be accomplished to guarantee business success.

Essential business activities are shaped by strategic, operational, and nondiscretionary elements required for corporate viability and long-term growth. Unsatisfactory performance of any of these essential activities produces less-than-desired overall business performance. In addition, these elements and essential business activities are dynamic, changing as a company grows. As they change, effective financial organizations will shift resources and services to meet emerging management needs. Failure to understand these essential business activities will result in a mismatch of operating needs with available financial services.

CREATING EFFECTIVE FINANCIAL ORGANIZATIONS

This book provides the tools for experienced financial professionals to leverage their technical expertise, judgment, and experience to improve the effectiveness of their financial organizations. The structured approach described in Chapter 2 and the lists of diagnostic attributes included in Chapters 3 through 8 permit a focused evaluation of financial services supporting essential business activities.

The structured approach for conducting a self-assessment provides a focused review at two levels. At one level, the self-assessment examines specific controllership responsibilities and activities. Using *service attribute* questionnaires, the self-assessment defines the structure and features within the scope of controllership services. Using *performance indicator* checklists, controllers summarize financial services quantitatively as a basis for evaluating the effectiveness of those activities to the organization.

At a second level, the structured approach directs attention to the control framework of the organization. Comprising the policies, organizational structure, and procedures that define the overall organization and the financial function, the control framework should allow effective execution and delivery of financial services that support an organization's essential business activities. Evaluating the control framework should enable the controller to detect flaws and to classify improvement opportunities for delivering financial services. Findings and recommendations resulting from this structured approach should become the basis for implementation plans.

2

CREATING EFFECTIVE FINANCIAL ORGANIZATIONS

Financial organizations anxious to respond effectively to management needs should conduct self-assessments to identify key improvement opportunities and to develop and execute action plans to exploit those opportunities. Effective self-assessments begin with commitment of senior financial management and cooperation of nonfinancial areas. Financial and nonfinancial personnel should expect to contribute extensively to self-assessment tasks, enabling management to determine:

- What financial services are needed but not received
- What financial services are received but not needed
- How effectively the financial organization delivers essential services

Consisting of six tasks, effective self-assessments use top-down approach and focus on essential financial services and information, which support strategic objectives. Since senior management officers have the strongest understanding of overall business strategy and the critical issues facing the organization, they can best establish self-assessment scope and priorities. Starting with this broad base, the self-assessment focus will shift to those limited, but essential, activities that must be accomplished to guarantee business success. Since all organizations operate within budget and resource limits, analyses, improvement opportunities, and action plans should target those key financial services and functional areas that support essential business activities.

TASK 1—ESTABLISHING SCOPE AND PRIORITIES

Self-assessments start by confirming management's understanding of three dimensions of the busines: strategy, organizational structure, and essential business activities. Tools to develop this understanding include strategic and operational plans, organizational charts, and key operating statistics. Management should be prepared to identify and characterize key issues by internal and external factors affecting business performance, as well as by business segments impacted and by the level of management concern. Internal factors classify under functions such as planning, marketing, sales, accounting, personnel, production, and materials. External factors could be classified broadly as arising from economic supplier, competitor, regulation, and technology impacts. Segments reflect how business activities logically classify and organize operations. For example, an energy and chemical company would segment activities under broad areas such as exploration and production, chemicals, and petroleum products.

Defining essential business activities narrows the self-assessment to a limited and manageable number of activities. Using input from financial and nonfinancial management, these essential activities should be limited to major business activities with large dollar involvement. Essential business activities are closely tied to major performance fluctuations and have significant value-added or value-lost impact. In addition, these activities correlate closely to key management issues and concerns.

TASK 2—IDENTIFYING ESSENTIAL BUSINESS PROCESSES

Identifying essential business processes moves the self-assessment to more focused and detailed analyses. This task uses business segments identified during Task 1 to identify primary and support business functions performed by each business segment. Functions include services such as human resources, distribution, materials management, and finance.

Each business function should reduce to four to eight business processes. Business processes are groups of logically related activities associated with producing products and services or managing resources. As an example, finance business processes would include accounting, financial planning, budgeting, and acquisition planning. Once identified, management determines essential business processes by identifying those processes most significant in supporting primary business functions and achieving essential business activities.

TASK 3—SPECIFYING KEY FINANCIAL SERVICES AND EXPECTATIONS

This task identifies specific financial services needed to achieve essential business activities. The analysis uses perceptions of financial and nonfinancial management to rank the significance and quality of financial services. Management assessments of the

11

expected and actual significance of financial services will point to possible service gaps and redundancies and should focus on those key financial services required to support essential business activities. Rankings should range from "no significance" to "high significance" of these services.

TASK 4—ASSESSING KEY FINANCIAL SERVICES

Management performs diagnostic reviews of key financial services by applying function-specific and control framework criteria to determine the effectiveness of existing services. These reviews require in-depth interviews with appropriate financial personnel. Chapters 4 through 8 include diagnostic questionnaires for service attributes for each major financial function. Chapter 4, Controlling, also includes performance indicator checklists for transaction processing activities. These questionnaires should be tailored or expanded to focus on those financial services supporting essential business activities.

Management also should evaluate financial services with respect to the control framework, consisting of policies, organization, and procedures. Chapter 3 includes questionnaires to apply these criteria. Using function-specific findings as a guide, management should determine financial services effectiveness by documenting where specific policies, organization, and procedures should change to better support strategic and management needs.

TASK 5—IDENTIFYING IMPROVEMENT OPPORTUNITIES

Using results from Task 4, management documents improvement opportunities by type, such as policy, procedure, or organizational change. Formal plans should translate these opportunities into specific implementation tasks. These plans should define and assign responsibilities, set timetables, and establish measurable goals for each implementation task.

Since successful implementation will require an investment of authority and resources at top management, findings and implementation plans should be presented for management review and approval. Knowledge of corporate management priorities should enable senior management to assign priorities and to recommend timing for implementation tasks. Senior management support ensures that staff, monetary, and other resources will be adequate for implementation needs.

TASK 6—IMPLEMENTING IMPROVEMENTS

For implementation activities, management must develop control schedules and status reporting systems to monitor implementation tasks. Implementation progress should be analyzed periodically to determine accomplishments and resolve problems. Control and reporting systems should include status meeting schedules, progress reporting formats, and issue resolution statements.

3

CONTROL FRAMEWORK

Controllers and chief financial officers complete their assessments of financial effectiveness when they move beyond a function-specific review to look at the larger control framework of their organization. The control framework includes the policies, organization, and procedures that dictate how the financial organization should work.

Assessing the control framework should consider:

- How effectively policies are established, communicated to employees, monitored, and enforced
- Whether organizational structure, productivity, staffing levels, and staff development are adequate to support business needs
- Whether procedures accurately reflect work flows, identify internal controls, and are effectively communicated to, and applied by, employees
- How effectively information systems support the financial function

POLICIES

To remain competitive in today's marketplace, organizations require a solid framework to plan, execute, and manage financial function activities. Strategic plans generally provide a foundation for such a framework. Implementing those strategies effectively requires appropriate policies and procedures to guide the execution of strategic directives. Since effective strategies are responsive to environmental change, policies and procedures must also be flexible to change. In this regard, policies and procedures should be designed to promote shifts in actions, behaviors, and practices to support changing strategies.

Policies and procedures, designed in concert with business strategies, enforce strategy implementation by:

- Promoting uniform handling of similar activities to optimize coordination of tasks and minimize redundancies
- Limiting independent actions by setting guidelines for the type and direction of actions to be taken
- Aligning actions and behaviors throughout an organization to strategies to minimize conflicting practices and promote a unified approach to strategy implementation
- Acting as an automatic decision maker by formalizing precedents for resolving issues.

When properly established and maintained, policies and procedures form the framework for institutionalizing strategy.

Guidelines and standards should be considered when reviewing corporate policies and procedures. Closely related to policies and procedures, guidelines and standards provide practical means for making policies and procedures operationally effective. As advisory or directional aids, guidelines fit standard procedures to specific circumstances. They offer specific examples of how a procedure will affect a specific job or activity. Guidelines, along with procedures, communicate to staff how things should be done.

Useful for evaluating compliance with policies and procedures, a standard should be a specific, objective, measurable reading, obtainable during the normal course of business. Characteristics of standards should be documented with respect to:

- Purpose, which describes the policy or procedure being measured
- Specific objective and measurable datum that indicates policy compliance
- Optimal value of the standard to conclude policy compliance
- Title of the position responsible for monitoring the standard
- Frequency recommended for monitoring the standard

A method for monitoring each standard should be defined, and a reporting mechanism established for deviations from standards. This mechanism should be capable of identifying escalating problems, as well as notifying individuals that their work is not up to standard.

When policies and procedures are impractical, corporate strategies cannot be effectively executed. Guidelines and standards provide practical methods to implement and control policies and procedures, contributing to the overall effectiveness of the financial function by facilitating strategy implementation.

An effectiveness review of policies should consider:

- Policy structure
- Implementation
- Maintenance

Policy Structure

For financial policies to succeed in supporting the critical business processes, they must contain enough information for specific guidance to roles and responsibilities of each area. Describing "what should be done," policy documents should:

- Briefly describe the intent of the policy
- Summarize the issues, reasons, and conditions forming the basis of the policy
- Discuss the significant results that the policy statement seeks to produce
- Identify the organizational units affected by the policy
- Indicate responsibility for implementing and maintaining conditions set forth by the policy
- Identify existing company documentation supporting the policy statement

The chief financial officer generally retains authority to issue policy, although the authority may be delegated to managers responsible for the functional areas where specific policies apply. Responsibility for the process of maintaining policies should be clearly defined. A policy statement regarding the format for documentation of policies should be clearly stated.

Implementation

Policy effectiveness depends on management success in implementing policies. Well-designed communications programs ensure that employees understand existing policies, have timely information on policy changes, and understand whether they comply with policies.

Best understood if documented thoroughly and organized logically, policies should be grouped into manuals directed toward particular audiences. For each audience, manuals may be compiled based on staff level or organizational unit depending on the size of the company. For a large company, a hierarchy of policy documentation may include:

- *Companywide policy manual,* containing company directives and a summary of the other manuals in the hierarchy. The primary audience is companywide executives with cost-center responsibility.
- *Functionwide policy manual,* containing policies, guidelines, and standards that describe company positions on matters of development or operation of activities within the function. The primary audience is functionwide management.
- *Department manuals,* defining policy for the internal operations of a department. The primary audience is the department staff.

Training programs linking policies to strategic directives and interpreting their meaning to a particular organizational unit are important for policy deployment. Inadequate training may produce failure of an otherwise high-quality set of policies.

Maintenance

As economic, corporate, and market environments change, strategies will change and require review and possible modification to policies. Dynamic environments dictate timely approval and implementation of policy changes.

To detect policy obsolescence, particularly if departments reorganize or department management changes, responsibility for monitoring policies should be centrally maintained. However, responsibility for policy maintenance should be allocated to the appropriate managers of each functional area. User areas responsible for preparing documentation should receive training and assistance as needed.

Steps for maintaining policies should be documented in the policy manual and should:

- Identify the organizational unit responsible for policies maintenance
- Serve as a guide for documentation activities
- Ensure that changes to policy statements are reviewed, approved, and prepared in a standard format
- Provide basic documentation guidance to individuals with documentation responsibilities

POLICIES ATTRIBUTES

1. Do financial policies support implementation of corporate strategies?
2. Do financial policies address each financial function (controlling, performance reporting, treasury, internal audit, and tax)?
3. Are policy statements timely and of adequate quality?
4. Do policies satisfy the related elements of business needs, management objectives, and any management agreements?
5. Are policies complete according to the standard components of a policy statement?
6. Is policy language clear and understandable?
7. Is there consistency between components of a policy with respect to:

    a. Purpose and background?
    b. Objectives?
    c. Consistency of scope?
    d. Responsibility of the policy?

  8. Are policies, which address ratios or other economic indicators, stated to allow for changes in the financial environment without requiring that policies be revised?

  9. Do procedures and activities required by financial policies conflict with existing policies in other functional areas, such as marketing or production?

10. Is the chief financial officer responsible for review and final approval of all financial policies?

11. Do independent auditors review significant management controls for selected policies, guidelines, and standards?

12. Do managers of each user area review and approve new policies to ensure that these policies:
    a. Are supported by the results of a policy review?
    b. Satisfy business needs and management objectives?
    c. State the policy clearly and concisely?

13. Does a group responsible for policy maintenance monitor and coordinate documentation activities throughout the company?

14. Do objectives of the documentation group ensure:
    a. Consistent use of a standardized approach for documenting policies throughout the company?
    b. Effective review of all policies?
    c. The proper coordination of all policy documentation activities?

15. Do responsibilities of the policy maintenance group include:
    a. Establishing a consistent and standardized documentation approach?

b. Establishing methods to monitor documentation activities?

c. Recommending documentation priorities to management?

d. Preparing a master plan for documentation activities?

e. Coordinating and monitoring documentation projects?

f. Providing assistance and documentation expertise to areas with documentation projects?

g. Assisting in the ongoing maintenance of documentation?

h. Performing special projects as requested by company management?

i. Refraining from preparing documentation for user areas except under special circumstances?

j. Refraining from performing internal audit functions?

16. Do responsibilities in the documenting policy include:

a. User areas responsible for reviewing policies and standards, and for preparing documentation?

b. Managers of each user area responsible for review and approval of new policies and standards?

c. Chief financial officer for review and final approval of all policies?

d. Independent auditors responsible for review of significant management controls for selected policies and standards?

17. Are policy manuals compiled in accordance with the corporate organization structure?

18. Are manuals distributed according to the physical location of the readers, and does the physical structure of the manual follow the organizational structure of the department?

19. Are manuals organized to address the various levels of management and policy responsibility?

20. If there is a companywide manual, does it:

    a. Articulate corporate strategies?

    b. Summarize other manuals in the hierarchy?

21. If there is a functionwide policy manual, does it describe the company position on matters of general interest concerning planning and development of operation within the function?

22. If there are department manuals, do they contain:

    a. Policies, guidelines, and standards for the internal operations of the department?

    b. Detailed procedures for the department?

    c. A reference showing the organization of the department?

23. Are numbering schemes sufficiently flexible to identify:

    a. Type of function?

    b. Type of manual?

    c. Section of manual?

    d. Policy, guideline, or standard number?

24. Are policies numbered with corresponding policies and corresponding numbers? Do related procedures have corresponding numbers?

25. Do employees understand policies applicable to them, as well as the meaning of those policies?

26. Are policy changes communicated with timeliness to all affected employees?

27. Is feedback on policy compliance effectively communicated to all employees?

28. Are training programs used to communicate policy to employees in a manner appropriate to the level of the employee?

29. Are inputs to the policy formulation monitored for:

    a. Economic environment?

    b. Corporate environment?

    c. Market environment?
    d. Regulatory environment?

30. Is compliance with existing policies monitored?
31. Are causes for noncompliance identified?
32. Are corresponding guidelines and standards evaluated?
33. What is the role of internal and external auditors in recommending policy change?
34. Are policies reviewed and changed regularly?
35. Are documentation activities planned?
36. Does a policy review process consider:
    a. Assignment of review tasks?
    b. Appropriateness of overall review organization?
    c. Role of internal audit?
    d. Documentation of new policy and standards?
    e. Circularization for comment?
    f. Compliance with standard formats?
    g. Acceptance mechanism?
    h. Publication?
    i. Follow-through development of related procedures, standards, and guidelines?
    j. Monitoring and control of each documentation project, including scheduled progress reporting?
37. Is policy manual issuance controlled with respect to:
    a. distributing and recording the location of policy manuals?
    b. Maintaining control logs and distribution lists of manual holders?

ORGANIZATION

The financial function relies on the individuals comprising the financial staff to execute services effectively. Personal qualities, as well as technical and communication skills, should enable the financial staff to balance active involvement as a decision support resource with objectivity and independence. Organizational structure and policies provide an environment to challenge and reward staff and individual efforts. An effectiveness review of the financial organization should consider:

a. Organizational structure
b. Staff productivity
c. Staff development

Organizational Structure

Research to define an optimum organizational structure has suggested that there is no one "best" way to organize an operation. Organizational design or structure should be tailored to each situation. The most suitable structure for a given financial function organization depends on the internal and external environment affecting it.

To provide benefits to operational units, good organizational structures:

- Clearly identify individual responsibility and authority
- Group similar business activities and duties into logical organizational functions
- Dispose of jurisdictional conflicts between individuals
- Prevent duplication
- Decrease likelihood of "runarounds"
- Make communication easier by keeping channels clear
- Identify promotional opportunities encouraging executive development
- Provide basis for performance appraisal and individual capabilities

- Aid wage and salary administration
- Permit operating expansion with adequate control

In most organizations, the financial function provide input into operating and strategic decision-making processes. Concurrently, the financial function has fiduciary responsibility for accurate internal and external financial reporting and for safeguarding assets. This fiduciary responsibility requires the financial function to maintain independence from operating management.

Because of conflicting operating management obligations, the financial function is challenged to balance these dual roles.

Evaluating financial function effectiveness requires assessing the risks associated with operational involvement and determining whether existing controls are capable of preserving objectivity and independence.

Staff Productivity

Since financial function expenses are largely for staff salaries, staff productivity is a key element in determining the effectiveness of the financial function. The financial function achieves optimum productivity by coordinating activities and tasks with proper staffing levels within appropriate spans of control.

Excessive layers of personnel are costly; hamper communication, planning, and control; and adversely affect morale. Functions performed at the lower levels of an organization are usually grouped according to similarity of activities. At higher levels, groupings relate to the interaction and exchange of information by management. Appropriate combinations of activities provide adequate internal control though segregation of duties. Well-structured activities improve staff utilization and may create economies of scale.

Reviewing procedures to perform financial activities is as important as analyzing the grouping of organizational activities. Procedures should represent the most efficient process for achieving desired results. Using work simplification techniques, each step of a procedure should be assessed to determine whether it could be combined with another step, simplified, or eliminated. Additionally, work standards for each activity should form a basis for staffing-level decisions, as well as performance monitoring and evaluation. Established work standards specify the amount of time required for an experienced employee to complete a job when following a prescribed method. Reviewing standards and their use by the financial organization is essential for assessing organizational effectiveness.

In many organizations, staffing levels evolve in reaction to various internal factors rather than as the result of an approved plan. Factors influencing staffing levels include:

- Staff availability, ability, and experience
- Variety and nature of staff activities
- Delegated authority
- Existence of policies and procedures
- Rate of business change
- Business schedules and timetables

An inappropriate mix of staff capabilities and support actually may hamper productivity, as well as produce redundancies and gaps in functional responsibility.

Many organizations staff the financial function to meet peak workload requirements. Overtime is typically an alternative to meeting these demands. The financial activities of most organizations follow a combination of workload patterns that include:

- Routine functions
- Cycle-intense functions
- Random-intense functions

Routine functions include activities such as payroll, customer billing, accounts receivable, and accounts payable. These activities often follow a reasonably uniform pattern of work throughout the year peaking toward the end of each accounting period.

A cycle-intense pattern refers to certain, predictable periods of the year involving significant increases in the financial staff workload. In addition to the month-end and year-end increases in routine work, cycle-intense activities may include monthly, quarterly, and yearly financial closings and analytical review. Profit planning and budget preparation and analysis are cycle-intense activities that can significantly increase staff workload.

Random-intense activities such as acquisitions, special financial analyses, and capital expenditure planning can increase workload significantly at unexpected times during the year.

Achieving optimum staffing levels requires consideration of peak workload requirements, as well as the organizational activities to be performed.

Span of control directly affects staff productivity. Span of control refers to the number of individuals who report to a manager, as well as the number of activities for which the manager is responsible. Productivity among financial staff members is optimized when the span of control enables responsible managers to effectively manage, motivate, and evaluate performance of employees. As a result, the appropriate span of control will depend on the abilities of managers and subordinates.

The span of control framework affects the shape of an organization and its communication channels. A relatively flat organization, which results from wide spans of control, shortens the communication channel from top to bottom. It may foster general supervision since managers may not be able to devote significant time to individual staff members. In contrast, narrow spans of control allow for close supervision but lengthen communication channels and may increase cost.

Staff Development

An effective financial function depends on finding, hiring, and retaining individuals with the capability and motivation to perform in a complex environment. Staffing jobs with the right individuals is a dynamic process. Proper staffing matches characteristics of the position and the individual. A company developing a strong financial function can recruit from other companies with reputations for having strong financial functions or develop its own talent. One approach requires assimilating individuals into an established corporate culture. The second approach is time-consuming and requires a substantial commitment of resources. Effective staff developing begins with recruiting activities and encompasses initial placement, career development, and training.

An effective recruiting and selection process relies on the exchange of valid, accurate information about candidate and organization. Ideal candidates should have appropriate educational or professional backgrounds, such as undergraduate or graduate degrees in accounting, finance, or economics, or should be CPAs with a business background. Candidates should provide evidence of interpersonal skills and other relative attributes. In addition, managers should supply accurate job descriptions, requirements, and expectations.

The initial experiences in an organization are particularly important in shaping a long-term relationship between the individual and the organization. Initial placement should provide development of individual business skills and should improve technical skills in relation to the individual's background. Staff members should have realistic information, challenging work, and effective supervision.

Individual development is a vital part of supporting staff and increasing the effectiveness of financial services. Effective career development systems should consist of structured career paths supported by well-designed training, continuing education programs, and proficient personnel evaluation practices. Career paths should provide for promotions that expose financial staff members to other aspects of the company's operation in order to broaden their business experience and improve their communication and technical skills. Career development should strive to match an individual's career aspirations with opportunities for achieving them. Moving financial personnel between corporate offices and divisions or operating units could be part of the career path design. Lateral transfers to other functional areas of the company also may enhance an individual's opportunities for advancement.

Influencing individual motivation and capability to perform specific jobs, training and educational programs typically promote better performance. Training programs should place special emphasis on developing interpersonal skills and balancing the dual roles of the financial function. Training should include company-sponsored and outside technical programs. As for backup support in the event of absenteeism or turnover, cross-training is a productive way to broaden an individual's knowledge of a function.

Successful development of financial staff members relies on the financial manager's ability to fairly and accurately assess an individual's working characteristics and performance. Not all staff will possess or develop the necessary skills required for long-term success. Some characteristics are difficult to assess during the initial selection process and must be judged on the basis of subsequent performance. Effective personnel evaluation system should provide formal analysis of an individual's performance on the job, as well as constructive feedback, to ensure that performance is sustained, modified, or improved. An evaluation program not only monitors the development of staff members, but also should provide historical information to assess what skills are required for long-term success in each job.

ORGANIZATION ATTRIBUTES

1. Is the organization's mission or purpose clearly defined?
2. Is the mission statement for all functional organizations prepared annually?
3. Are mission statements updated quarterly?
4. Are responsibilities clearly defined and documented at all levels?
5. Is responsibility coupled with corresponding authority?
6. Are assigned functions and respective staffing reasonable?
7. Do staff members report to only one superior?
8. Are lines of authority within the organization clearly defined?
9. Is individual authority clearly defined?
10. Is absolute responsibility for acts of subordinates assigned to higher authority?
11. Is authority properly delegated?
12. Are levels of authority maintained at a minimum?
13. Are reporting relationships clearly defined and understood?
14. Are reporting relationships structured to perform functions effectively?
15. Are reporting relationships clearly structured to avoid staff confusion?
16. Will planned changes to functional areas outside the financial function have an impact on the financial function?

17. What are the general attitudes toward change within the organization?

18. Does the financial function participate in operating business decisions by:
    a. Presenting information and analyses?
    b. Offering guidance and advice?
    c. Monitoring progress against plans?
    d. Challenging plans and actions?
    e. Recommending actions?

19. Does the financial function participate in strategic business decisions by:
    a. Presenting information and analyses?
    b. Offering guidance and advice?
    c. Monitoring progress against plans?
    d. Challenging plans and actions?
    e. Recommending actions?

20. Are there advantages to changing the financial function role in operating or strategic decision making?

21. What are the service expectations of providers and recipients of financial services?

22. What are managerial expectations regarding the financial function role when key decisions are made for critical business processes?

23. Are there advantages to changing the financial function role when key decisions are made in critical business processes?

24. What responsibility does the financial function assume for:
    a. Annual planning and budgeting?
    b. Long-range planning?
    c. Capital-expenditure planning?
    d. Periodic budget reviews?
    e. Narratives of operations?

    f. Personnel evaluations?

    g. Incentive compensation?

25. What degree of decision-making authority (full, primary, or equal) do line and staff functions maintain over:

    a. Hiring?

    b. Transfer?

    c. Promotion?

    d. Termination?

    e. Salary adjustment?

    f. Bonus?

    g. Setting work priorities?

26. Are there advantages to changing established lines of authority?

27. Are there duplicate or overlapping activities between the financial organization and other areas?

28. Have positions been established in response to:

    a. Discovery of fraud?

    b. Defalcation?

    c. Illegal payments?

    d. Unexpected write-off of inventory or receivables?

29. Do opportunities exist to increase staff productivity or reduce workloads by:

    a. Developing or improving computer-based systems?

    b. Contracting out nonrecurring work?

    c. Contracting out routine work?

    d. Eliminating functions?

    e. Consolidating functions?

    f. Rescheduling activities?

    g. Reducing the frequency of activities?

30. What are staff-meeting procedures with respect to:

    a. Timing?

    b. Attendance?

    c. Duration?

    d. Context?

31. Are there financial areas requiring improved financial and operating controls to enhance the company's overall profitability?

32. Are there current activities of the financial organization that could be eliminated or performed elsewhere without adversely affecting the company's internal controls?

33. Can financial procedures currently be simplified and made more efficient?

34. Are work standards established and is employee performance measured against these standards?

35. Are current activities of the financial organization redundant due to the advent of computer-based information systems?

36. Have staff positions within the financial organization been created for reasons other than increasing workloads or new responsibilities?

37. Have inappropriate levels of personnel (numbers or types) been assigned to perform activities within the financial organization?

38. Is each staff member's workload reasonably confined to perform a single function?

39. Are staffing levels appropriate for the time and frequency of special projects?

40. Are skill levels appropriate for the functions performed?

41. Are individuals frequently overly qualified for assigned tasks?

42. What existing constraints prevent or deter improved staff utilization?

43. What are the opportunities to interchange staff to increase utilization?

44. Where can capital expenditures be made to reduce operating costs and enhance staff productivity?

45. How does management philosophy impact on the size and cost-effectiveness of the financial function?

46. Is routine and repetitive work so fragmented that unjustified higher level staff perform it?

47. How do peak workloads or seasonality affect work utilization?

48. What additional resources would allow additional projects to be undertaken?

49. Could alternative levels of management enhance staff productivity within the financial organization?

50. How many positions are routinely coordinated by a single manager?

51. Are staff utilization reports or time analyses used as managerial tools?

52. What are the longer term costs and impacts on the financial function if no efforts are made to improve staff productivity?

53. Where can managers "stretch" through assuming a wider span of control by supervising more than one function?

54. Where is more management attention required to protect assets or enhance profitability?

55. Does personnel documentation include:
    a. Current and complete job descriptions?
    b. Minimum educational and experience requirements?
    c. Unique job factors, such as annual overtime and promotability?

56. Are the following appropriate:
    a. The level of management responsible for hiring?
    b. Interview procedures?
    c. Formal orientation programs?

57. Are counselors assigned to each staff member?

58. Are regular performance evaluations conducted?

59. What internal and external training programs are used?

PROCEDURES

Procedures document the approved steps to perform an activity. They always should be consistent with corporate policy.

Procedure Structure and Content

Procedures should contain enough information to describe the steps required to complete an activity in a manner consistent with corporate policy. Although procedure formats vary by company, every procedure should consist of several standard components. Effective procedures should clearly identify objective and scope in a narrative format as a reference for readers. They should identify the input sources that trigger the steps within a procedure. Input may include hard copy documents or events such as monthly cutoff. Output generated from procedure steps also should be identified with its destination(s). Procedure steps should include the title of the person responsible for completion. The bulk of a procedure should present detailed instructions for performing specific tasks. If company procedure formats permit, each procedure should include complete samples of each input/output document along with its source or destination. Each procedure should have an effective date, standard review date, and approval signature.

Approved procedures should be consolidated in a manual for distribution as an ongoing reference. For large companies, the hierarchy of procedure documentation may be structured to parallel the organization's lines of authority. The arrangement of the procedure manuals should be consistent with reporting relationships, responsibility assignments, and authority limitations of key individuals in each group.

Department procedure manuals contain the detailed procedures for a specific department with department staff as the primary audience. Department manuals also may contain policies for the department's internal operations and accepted criteria or measures of performance. The department manual may document a departmental organization, including a complete set of job descriptions.

Training for Procedures Implementation

To implement procedures successfully, users should have initial and ongoing training. Training will ensure that employees understand existing procedures, have timely information on changes, and understand how well they are complying with the approved procedures. Training programs to present procedures and provide feedback to management are essential to procedure development. Lack of or inadequate training can cause the failure of otherwise high-quality procedures.

Procedure Maintenance

Financial procedures require review and update over time. A maintenance process should enable changes to be approved, implemented, and communicated in a timely manner within the financial function. This process should minimize disruption and confusion within the organization. Procedures maintenance should be documented in the procedures manual. This documentation should:

- Identify the organizational unit responsible for procedure maintenance
- Ensure that procedures are reviewed, approved, and prepared in a standard format
- Provide basic documentation guidelines to individuals within the organization with documentation responsibilities

To prevent procedures from becoming obsolete, responsibility for the manual should be assigned so that it is not neglected in the event of reorganization or management change.

Procedures should be grouped into manuals by their intended audiences. Manuals may be compiled for a particular staff level, an organizational unit, or both, depending on company size. For a large company, a hierarchy for procedure documentation may be structured to parallel the organization. The arrangement of the manuals should be consistent with reporting relationships, responsibility assignments, and authority limitations of key individuals in each group.

PROCEDURES ATTRIBUTES

1. Do financial function procedures reflect the policies and standards of the company?
2. Do procedures include specific guidance as to roles and responsibilities?
3. Are all procedures complete according to standard components of a procedure?
4. Is procedure language clear and understandable?

5. Is there consistency between components of a procedure with respect to:

    a. Purpose and overview?
    b. Objectives?
    c. Consistency of scope?
    d. Responsibility of the procedure?

6. Are procedures organized as a set of steps needed to perform a task, and not as job descriptions for a particular person?

7. Are procedures or guidelines for ratios or other economic indicators stated to recognize changes in the financial environment without requiring that the documentation be edited?

8. Does the group responsible for procedure maintenance also monitor and coordinate all documentation activities throughout the company?

9. Do objectives of the documentation group include ensuring:

    a. Consistent use of standardized approach for documenting all procedures?
    b. Effective review of all procedures?
    c. Proper coordination of all documentation activities?

10. Do responsibilities for procedure maintenance include:

    a. Establishing a consistent and standardized documentation approach?
    b. Establishing methods to monitor all documentation activities?
    c. Recommending documentation priorities to management?
    d. Preparing a master plan for all documentation activities?
    e. Coordinating and monitoring documentation projects?
    f. Providing assistance and documentation expertise to areas with documentation projects?

    g. Performing special projects as requested by company management?

    h. Refraining from preparing documentation for user areas except under special circumstances?

    i. Refraining from performing internal audit functions?

11. Do other participants in the documentation process include:

    a. Users responsible for preparing and reviewing procedures, guidelines, and job descriptions?

    b. Managers of each user area responsible for reviewing and approving new procedures, guidelines, and job descriptions?

    c. Managers of the function responsible for review and final approval of all procedures, guidelines, and job descriptions?

    d. Independent auditors who review controls within procedures?

12. Is the chief financial officer responsible for review and final approval of all procedures?

13. Do independent auditors responsible review significant management controls for selected procedures?

14. Do managers of each user area review and approve new procedures to assure that they:

    a. Are supported by the results of a procedure review?

    b. Satisfy business needs and management objectives?

    c. State the procedure clearly and concisely?

15. Does the procedures manual structure parallel the organization of the company?

16. Are manuals divided into separate volumes according to the physical location of users?

17. Are manuals divided into separate volumes addressing the various levels and responsibilities of users?

18. Do department manuals contain:
    a. Policies of the internal operations of the department?
    b. Detailed procedures, guidelines, and standards for the department?
    c. A reference showing the organization of the department?
    d. A complete set of job descriptions?

19. Are numbering schemes sufficiently flexible to identify:
    a. Type of function?
    b. Type of manual?
    c. Section of manual?
    d. Policy, guideline, or standard number?

20. Are procedures, guidelines, and standards numbered to correspond to each other?

21. Do employees understand and can they perform procedures that apply to them?

22. Are changes in procedures communicated with timeliness to all affected employees?

23. Is feedback on procedures compliance effectively communicated to all employees?

24. Do training programs communicate procedures to employees, in a manner appropriate to the level of the employee?

25. Do training programs include refresher courses for existing and new employees?

26. If jobs exist that do not relate to an existing procedure, does this situation suggest obsolete job descriptions, or job descriptions providing *de facto* procedures?

27. Are processes used to monitor outside factors such as regulatory change, which are inputs to the procedure formulation process?

28. Do changes in strategic direction and corporate policy prompt changes or additions to current company procedures?

29. Do internal and external auditors recommend procedural changes?

30. Are procedures reviewed regularly?

31. Is procedure manual issuance controlled with respect to:
    a. Distributing and recording the location of procedure manuals?
    b. Maintaining control logs and distribution lists of manual holders?

4

CONTROLLING

THE CONTROLLING FUNCTION

The controlling function supports dual, but complementary, roles in an organization. The traditional controlling role includes financial reporting and internal control activities. Focused on maintaining effective transaction processing systems, the controlling function ensures that financial information is processed efficiently and with adequate controls to safeguard assets. In this role, the controller has responsibility for the integrity of general accounting and subsidiary systems.

As managers at all organizational levels increasingly demand accurate, integrated, and timely financial and operating reporting, the controlling role has broadened beyond accumulating, recording, and reporting financial information. Controllers must apply their financial expertise as a decision resource to management. Because management still requires a sound control and reporting framework, controllers face the challenge of balancing the needs for independence necessary to ensure financial information accuracy and integrity with their expanding decision support role.

An effective review of the controlling function should consider:

- Decision support services
- Transaction processing services

The controlling function fulfills its dual role through accounting, planning, analysis, and reporting activities. These activities should be integrated for functional and internal control. The controlling function should participate in establishing standards and identifying variances and also should have responsibility for the integrity of all financial data used for internal and external reporting.

An effectiveness review of the controllership's decision support role should focus on each functional area linked to the organization's essential business activities. Since this decision support role may be new for many controllers, the focus of this review should be on identifying service gaps and redundancies, as well as targeting services to be expanded.

An effectiveness review of decision support activities should consider:

- Planning
- Capital budgeting
- Operational budgeting and expenditure control
- Cost accounting and cost management
- Financial analysis
- Acquisitions and divestitures
- Special projects

Planning

Management depends on the planning function to prepare rational action plans for the future that anticipate financial consequences of current decisions. Planning enables management to take advantage of opportunities as they arise and to anticipate and react to changes impacting the business.

The objectives of evaluating the planning function include determining that:

- Plans are prepared according to management directives
- The variety of plans are adequately integrated
- Plans contain sufficient information to monitor and manage the business

Companies use long-range and operating plans to document strategic direction and near-term activities. Long-range plans should encompass a sufficient time horizon to forecast the results of implementing the business strategy. Effective long-range plans emerge through an understanding of customers, competitors, and environmental factors, as well as company strengths and weaknesses. These plans should include probability analyses for key assumptions. Operating plans govern the interactions between major organizational groups. They should be based on goals and objectives of the operating units and should identify and justify resource requirements.

Effective planning requires top management commitment to review and support all plans. Plans should describe and be consistent with organizational goals and objectives. They should be integrated in terms of key assumptions, objectives, and approach used to develop the plans. Planning should include analyses of the impact of changes in key assumptions and nonmonetary performance measures.

Responsibilities for plan preparation should be well defined to ensure clear accountability. Planning procedures should be documented. Planning personnel should understand their role and responsibilities. Responsibilities for providing the key assumptions and components of each financial plan should be established. Controls should exist to ensure proper integration of plan assumptions and changes.

Plans should clearly identify assumptions and variables to enable management to assess the relative success of the plan or the need to revise plans based on changes in those assumptions or variables. Plan detail will vary according to planning horizon. At the most detailed level, the coding of plan input should be consistent with the chart of accounts. Plans should have sufficient flexibility to accommodate revisions when assumptions change and to allow multiple methods of aggregation, various reporting periods, and multiple planning levels.

Capital Budgeting

Capital budgeting is essentially the execution of plans, prepared during the strategic planning process, to meet corporate requirements. As a component of the planning function, capital budgeting focuses on controlling project expenditures and cash flow.

The objectives of evaluating the capital-budgeting process are to determine how well the budgeting system:

- Assists management in selecting assets to acquire by providing logical, descriptive, and quantitative techniques for analyzing capital-acquisition alternatives
- Establishes and maintains control over all approved capital expenditures while ensuring optimal use of spendable resources

- Sets and monitors performance standards for capital acquisitions

A systematic approach to investment analysis gives management a meaningful basis for selecting among investment opportunities. The chief financial officer is ultimately responsible for economic evaluation of investment alternatives. Information for this evaluation should include project descriptions and estimates of earning power, documented by descriptive and quantitative evidence. Analytic techniques, including discounted cash flows and internal rates of return may form the quantitative analysis.

Approval levels for capital expenditures should be based on materiality. Line management may have authority to approve minor capital additions and routine maintenance, but major plant expansion should require approval from a steering committee or the board of directors. Optimal use of spendable resources requires that capital plans encompass a sufficient planning horizon. Investments should be classified by type, such as required, discretionary, replacement, and expansion investments.

Controlling capital expenditures should be similar to controlling budgets for operating expenses. The monitoring process should include status reporting for costs and completion dates. Overruns should be reported to appropriate management, and material deviations from estimated budgets should be explained. If necessary, new limits should be recommended and approved.

Operational Budgeting and Expenditure Control

Well-designed budgeting and expenditure control processes are essential for monitoring managerial and operational performance. These systems should supply the information to update initial plans, analyze trends, and communicate current results to all levels of the organization.

The objectives of evaluating the budgeting and expenditure control process include determining if:

- Budgets are prepared according to management directives and support corporate objectives and policies
- Budgets for operational units are integrated
- Responsibility for ongoing expenditure control is clearly defined to ensure accountability

Annual budgets are a planning tool, as well as a vehicle for control. They should be consistent with corporate goals and objectives, and meet with management approval. Effective budgeting should be proactive and goal-oriented, enabling the budgeting process to support directly the tactical aspects of corporate planning.

As with all plans, annual operating budgets should be integrated among organizational units. Well-documented preparation procedures support effective plan integration by establishing a consistent approach for each organizational component to develop its plan. A strict timetable for budget preparation promotes coordination of required activities to develop a consolidated corporate budget. Integration ensures consistency and efficiency and promotes communication between related areas.

Responsibility for budget preparation and subsequent expenditure control should be specifically defined. Clearly defined responsibilities promote accountability while motivating individuals to meet corporate goals. Defined responsibility is the foundation for updating plans, monitoring trends, communicating results, and correcting problems in a timely manner.

Cost Accounting and Cost Management

A company's management must understand its total product or service costs and the related production and organizational activities that impact those costs. Cost management systems need to provide this cost information to manage operations cost, reduce product or service costs, and price products and services.

The objectives of evaluating cost accounting and cost management information systems include determining that

- Accurate product and service costs are developed and updated
- Cost systems support product pricing activities
- Operations performance measurement applies cost information to monitor essential business activities
- Cost management recognizes product life cycles
- Management receives concise and timely cost reporting
- Cost management, financial, operations, and manufacturing systems are sufficiently integrated

Effective cost systems develop accurate product or service costs because all cost information objectives and functions rely on accurate costs. Effective cost systems should also identify activities that impact costs. Traditional cost assignment activities have included direct labor, production units, and machine time. Many companies have begun to measure the impact of other activities such as material ordering, engineering changes, and product complexity.

The cost system should support product pricing activities by providing accurate product costs. Inaccurate product costs can result in lost business due to overpricing or in retention of unprofitable businesses or product lines.

Cost management systems should support operations performance measurement to ensure that essential business activities are adequately monitored. These performance measures may be financial and statistical and should include activities that impact product cost, quality, and delivery performance. Successful cost reduction programs depend on accurate product costs and an understanding of activities that drive those costs. Cost management systems also should receive feedback on profitability for management to identify successful products and services.

Cost management should be sensitive to product life cycles. Management must understand development and capital costs as well as learning curve efficiencies to sustain profitability over the life span of a product and its offshoots.

Effective cost management systems should provide concise management reporting with data summarized appropriately for each management level. Cost management systems should integrate to the company's financial, operations, and manufacturing systems for management reliance on data integrity. Management reporting should focus on cost drivers, delivery performed, and quality measures linked to the organization's essential business activities. Reporting formats should show accountability, forcing appropriate management to take corrective action as needed.

Financial Analysis

Financial analysis activities of the controlling function comprise the follow-up tasks to planning and budget preparation activities. Financial analysis includes retrospective and prospective viewpoints and provides the basis for many managerial decisions.

The objectives of evaluating the financial analysis activities include determining how:

- Variances against plans are monitored as actual results are reported
- Actual results and impacts are linked to all other plans

Management's ability to monitor planning and budgeting activities is affected by comparing actual results to original plans.

Key variances should be identified promptly and communicated throughout the organization. Unit managers should develop initial analyses, with findings reflected in subsequent analyses and plans. When major variances are communicated to top management, corrective or supportive action should be taken and required budget modifications made.

Financial analysis results should be reflected in all plans with regard to financing decisions and anticipated cost of capital. Financial analysis procedures should be defined particularly in the areas of capital allocation and calculation of costs and through the use of sensitivity analysis and financial planning.

Acquisitions and Divestitures

Analysis of acquisitions and divestitures is primarily governed by corporate philosophy. Not present in all organizations, the strategic plan of an organization will dictate the need for this function.

The objectives of evaluating the acquisitions and divestiture function include evaluating the:

- Basis for the acquisition and divestiture philosophy
- Types of analyses performed to evaluate acquisition and divestiture candidates

Criteria to identify and analyze potential candidates should be linked to the strategic plan and have management approval. The criteria should be reviewed and updated as corporate and economic environments change. An effective acquisition and divestiture function should have strong internal communications, knowledge of corporate plans, and external communications with the investment community to assist in identifying potential candidates.

Analysis of acquisition and divestiture candidates should use a defined structure and consistent approach to permit equal consideration of all alternatives. The analysis structure should permit assigning appropriate weights to key analysis features. The approach should have adequate methods to determine purchase and sale prices. A strong analysis structure and approach should enable management to assess the impacts of purchases and sales on financial performance, as well as on treasury, legal, tax, and marketing functions.

Following an acquisition or divestiture, reviews should be completed to assess whether financial and organizational impacts occurred as expected. Management should use follow-up reviews to evaluate and improve the analysis structure and approach, particularly if actual results vary consistently and significantly with expected outcomes.

Special Projects

The controlling function often includes personnel dedicated to performing special projects. Project complexity will vary, and requests for special projects may originate throughout an organization. Special projects might include a review of dividend policy, lease-versus-buy evaluations, and buy-versus-make analyses.

The objectives of evaluating the special projects function include determining how:

- Special project requests are directed to functional areas and coordinated with other departments
- Resources are committed to special projects

Channels to request special assistance should be clearly defined. Departmental coordination must exist to ensure effective execution of special projects, especially when priorities conflict. Large, complex projects may require steering committees or outside consultants. The structure of the special projects function, as well as the committed resources, should reflect project complexity and demand for special project services. Staffing should match technical skills, depth of experience, and functional responsibilities to project needs. Budgets should be developed with appropriate chargebacks to requesting departments.

DECISION SUPPORT ATTRIBUTES

Planning

1. Do plans present and evaluate all realistic alternatives?
2. Are plans developed according to management directives?
3. Does management approve and support all plans?
4. Are plans sufficiently detailed to manage and monitor business performance?
   a. Does the structure of forecasts conform to the chart of accounts?
   b. Do long-range plans describe corporate goals and objectives, operating policies, and key assumptions?
   c. Are units of measure used consistently and correctly?
   d. Are objectives quantified in terms of rate of return, market growth, and product development?
   e. Do assumptions reflect policy changes, capacity, labor requirements, market trends, and sales mix?
5. Is responsibility for plan preparation clearly defined to ensure accountability?
6. Is responsibility for developing key plan assumptions and components clearly defined?

7. Is responsibility for plan execution explicitly defined?

8. Are key planning assumptions clearly stated?

9. Are planning procedures formalized and documented?

10. Are plans integrated horizontally across departments and consolidated vertically by operating units?

11. Are plan revisions linked to the original plans?

12. Do long-range plans encompass a sufficient planning horizon to forecast the results of implementing strategy?

13. Do long-range plans include customer and competitor analyses and consider environmental factors and internal strengths and weaknesses?

14. Does long-range planning evaluate growth potential and market saturation of current and planned products?

15. Do operating plans clearly state goals and objectives for operating units?

16. Do operating plans specify resource requirements and provide economic justification?

17. Is the budgeting structure of operating plans consistent with the reporting structure in the operating units?

18. Are multiyear forecasts available by product or product line?

19. Do market analyses provide a basis for sales forecasts?

20. Do quantitative forecasting methods include trend, cycle and seasonal forecasting, as well as regression and correlation analyses?

21. Are plan and forecast updates timely? Does the planning cycle:
    a. Include formal schedules for plan preparation, review, and approval?
    b. Communicate schedule and input requirements to management, with adequate lead time to complete tasks?

22. Is the planning approach, such as top-down or bottom-up, consistent with management practices?

23. Does plan preparation use:
    a. Well-documented procedures to delineate plan development?
    b. Computer-based planning tools?
    c. Standardized forms to develop routine plan elements?
    d. Mathematical techniques, such as profitability and trend analyses?

24. Do plans incorporate accounting rules, characteristics, and constraints?

25. Are plans defined by management control elements, such as standard costs, labor hours, and selling prices?

26. Do plan structure and content conform to management and financial reporting systems:
    a. Do management reports reflect the impact of sales forecast changes on the budget and operating plans?
    b. Are profit centers accountable for their operations and production, as well as their profits?
    c. Do nonmonetary performance measures exist, such as personnel statistics, market share, and manufacturing rejection rates?
    d. Are historical data integrated to the financial modeling process?

27. Are plans sufficiently flexible? Does the planning process allow:
    a. Revisions to assumptions resulting in revised plans and forecasts?
    b. Multiple plan aggregation by product line and geographic territory?
    c. Identification of dependencies and assumptions and budget modifications as needed?

   d. Separation of variable from programmed costs?
   e. Information accumulated in monthly or quarterly segments?
   f. Multiple planning viewpoints such as optimistic, best estimate, and pessimistic?

Capital Budgeting

1. Is there a formal annual budgeting process that receives management approval?

2. Does the planning horizon encompass completion of moderate-length acquisitions?

3. Are capital budgets linked to facilities requirements and strategic plans?

4. Do capital budgets classify acquisitions as replacement or expansion and essential or discretionary expenditures?

5. Are capital budgets established within the limits of the company's capacity to grow, manage risk, and assume new obligations?

6. Are phased completion schedules used for all capital projects?

7. Are objective economic evaluation methods, such as discounted cash flows and internal rates of return, used to value proposed projects?

8. Are project risks identified and evaluated?

9. Is sensitivity analysis performed to test variations in key assumptions?

10. Are comprehensive project status reports prepared on a regular basis?

11. Does status reporting of project costs:
   a. Provide management with timely information regarding potential cost overruns?

    b. Provide sufficient data for adequate cash planning?

    c. Reveal problem areas promptly to permit timely corrective action?

    d. Check accuracy of project proposals?

    e. Ensure proper expenditure approval?

    f. Highlight progress against phased completion schedules?

12. Are postacquisition appraisals, which compare forecasted to actual costs and value, conducted for all capital projects?

Operational Budgeting and Expenditure Control

1. Do unit managers participate in budget preparation?

2. Does top management review and approve all budgets?

3. Is the budget development approach (top-down or bottom-up) consistent with managerial practices and corporate plans and objectives?

4. Are budget development procedures fully documented?

5. Are automated budgeting and modeling systems used?

6. Are standardized forms used to develop routine budget components?

7. If budgeting assumptions change, how quickly can revised budgets be prepared?

8. Are budget assumptions and dependencies clearly identified?

9. Are budgeting responsibilities clearly defined and documented within all organizational units?

10. Does budget preparation:

    a. Document plan revisions from submission to approval?

    b. Incorporate accounting rules, characteristics, and constraints?

    c. Follow a formal schedule for preparation, review, and approval of all plan forecasts?

11. Are operating budgets coordinated with capital budgets?

12. Are operating budgets consistent among organizational units?

13. Is the coding structure for budget line items consistent with the chart of accounts?

14. Are authorization levels for expenditures appropriate for the relative size of the expenditure request?

15. Are formal procedures in place to document expenditure requests?

16. Are automatic budget checks made to assure sufficient balance prior to posting expenses?

17. Do management reports reflect impact of sales forecast changes on budget and operating plans?

18. Are profit centers accountable for their operations and production, as well as their profits?

19. Are nonmonetary performance measures, such as personnel statistics, market share, and manufacturing reject rates, used to evaluate operations?

Cost Accounting and Cost Management

1. Are annual budgets used as the basis for cost control?

2. Do computer-based systems support data collection and consolidation in the budgeting process?

3. Is budget information integrated with the financial reporting system for comparison to actual results?

4. Are tailored budget reviews and control reports, which allow

various levels of management to review and revise aggregate budget data, utilized?

5. Are budget overhead rates used at the department level for each major cost account?

6. Is information provided for the following:
   a. Pricing and cost estimating decisions?
   b. Efficiency and/or yield reporting?
   c. Monitoring product cost changes?

7. Are bills of material or formulas established?

8. Are routines established?

9. Are the following items considered:
   a. Production royalties?
   b. Start-up costs?
   c. Idle plant costs?
   d. Tooling costs?

10. Are separate cost elements established for:
    a. Direct labor?
    b. Indirect labor?
    c. Material?
    d. Freight/duty?
    e. Outside processing?

11. Is overhead separately identified as variable and fixed?

12. Are production and labor reporting data recorded on the same source document?

13. Are labor hourly rates captured by:
    a. Plant?
    b. Cost center?
    c. Job class?
    d. Operation?
    e. Individual?

14. Is labor reporting information captured by:
    a. Assigned cost center?

    b. Actual cost center?
    c. Operation?
    d. Job (work order)?
    e. Product?
    f. Job class?

15. Are general ledger balances supported by perpetual inventory records?

16. Is there a single inventory record-keeping system for financial and manufacturing sytems integration?

17. Are actual costs accumulated on a work order basis by cost center?

18. Is the cost impact of engineering changes captured?

19. Is material usage by product and raw material provided for performance measurement?

20. Is purchasing performance measured on a per item basis?

21. Is purchase price performance by period compared to budget?

22. Are purchase price information and material cost history available by location on a vendor basis?

23. Is material usage and/or yield controlled on:
    a. A plantwide basis?
    b. A cost center basis?
    c. An operation basis within cost center?
    d. By specific raw material item within cost center or operation?
    e. A work order basis?

24. Are direct labor rates, utilization, and efficiency available for performance measurement?

25. Is indirect labor detailed by categories?

26. Are overhead spending and capacity utilization monitored?

27. Are costs included in areas other than direct production departments?

28. Are costs for nonproduction projects (e.g., maintenance, toolroom, capital projects, research) monitored?

29. Is equipment utilization monitored?

30. Are operating costs tracked on a machine-hour basis?

31. Are costs for setup and downtime monitored?

32. Are costs of quality (e.g., scrap, rework) identified and monitored?

33. Does the system support rapid changes to budgeted overheads in response to actual changes in volume?

34. Are flexible budgeting calculations used as part of a comprehensive financial reporting system?

35. Are service department costs allocated to production departments on a usage basis for cost visibility and control?

36. Does the cost allocation process support:
    a. Operating decisions for manufacturing management?
    b. Pricing decisions for marketing management?

37. Does the system apply overhead by:
    a. Labor dollar?
    b. Machine hour?
    c. Material?
    d. Other (as needed)?

38. Does the system allocate overhead from one department to another based on direct labor or other means?

39. Are revenue, cost, and contribution (margin) information with comparisons to budgets available to marketing and operational managers at appropriate levels?

40. Does the cost accounting system enable management to:
    a. Respond quickly to special requests for information?

    b. Control costs to improve productivity?

    c. Provide credible information for capital expenditure analysis?

    d. Manage return on investment objectives?

    e. Monitor the cost of quality?

    f. Ensure product quality and customer service?

    g. Assist engineers in making process and/or product improvements?

    h. Support engineers in developing cost estimates for new products?

    i. Control cash flow management?

    j. Support analysis for production introduction of new products?

    k. Support sourcing decisions for manufacturing products and materials?

    l. Manage product cost reduction programs?

41. Are transfer pricing practices among organizational units defined and understandable to management?

42. Are budget-to-actual cost comparisons made:

    a. For material, labor, and overhead by product or product lines?

    b. By organization for individual product or product lines?

43. Are financial reports for internal purposes prepared for:

    a. Direct costing?

    b. Full absorption costing?

    c. Direct and absorption costing basis?

44. Is there clear visibility over production and nonproduction costs?

45. Does reporting support analysis of cost trends?

46. Are margin trends monitored for major products?

47. Are productivity measures stressed?

48. Is reporting timely enough to be of use to operating management?

49. Does reporting support:
    a. Government contracting requirements?
    b. Activity-based product costing?

Financial Analysis

1. Do managers initiate variance analyses for their organizational units?
2. Do variance analyses aggregate upward and downward?
3. Are reasons for budget variances identified and categorized?
4. Do variance analyses initiate budget modifications?
5. Are favorable variances investigated to identify opportunities for performance improvement?
6. Are corrective actions taken in response to unfavorable variances?
7. Are current period, prior period, and year-to-date information reported for comparison?
8. Are financing decisions related to the overall corporate plan, capital expenditure plans, and operating cash needs?
9. Do financial analyses reflect cost of capital consistent with current and projected capital structure, as well as related costs of debt and equity?

Acquisitions and Divestitures

1. Is acquisition and divestiture policy linked to the corporate plan?
2. Are acquisition criteria explicit with respect to:
    a. Size?

    b. Ownership?
    c. Line of business?
    d. Geography?
    e. Regulatory considerations?
    f. Financial stability?
    g. Tax implications?
    h. Cash flow impact?
    i. Impact on overall financial condition?

3. Are divestiture criteria explicit with respect to:
    a. Cash flow?
    b. Profitability?
    c. "Fit" with corporate plan?

4. Are acquisition and divestiture criteria reviewed and updated periodically?

5. Is communication with the outside investment community adequate to assist in identifying acquisition and divestiture candidates?

6. Is a competent, internal team designated to evaluate potential acquisitions and divestitures?

7. Are operations, treasury, legal, marketing, accounting, and tax areas involved in evaluating acquisition and divestiture candidates?

8. Does the evaluation of acquisition and divestiture candidates include weighting for:
    a. Potential cash flow and earnings after acquisition or divestiture?
    b. Net asset value of target?
    c. Current and future market price of target?

9. Is a formal structure and approach used to analyze acquisition and divestiture candidates?

10. Are procedures established to price acquisition and divestiture candidates?

11. Is a format defined to present candidate analysis to management?

12. Are guidelines or procedures established to price divisions separately for potential divestiture?

13. Are follow-up reviews used to:
    a. Confirm the analysis of an acquisition's financial condition?
    b. Compare the actual financial and organizational impacts of the acquisition or divestiture against expected outcomes?

14. Are analysis structure and approach evaluated and revised if actual results vary consistently and significantly from expected outcomes?

Special Projects

1. Are channels of departmental communication clearly defined to request special project assistance?

2. Are formats and report content standardized where appropriate?

3. Are clear reporting lines established for all special projects?

4. Does project staffing match technical skills, depth of experience, and functional responsibilities to specific project needs?

5. Are project reporting procedures in place? Are these procedures followed?

6. Are studies completed and findings reported on time and within budget?

7. Are potential impacts of special projects on other departments evaluated and reported?

8. Are procedures in place for assessing priorities when multiple project requests conflict?

9. Are steering committees and status meetings used to monitor large projects?

10. Are time, money and other resource budgets set for each project?

11. Are postproject reviews conducted to report and analyze variances from project budget?

12. Are chargeback mechanisms in place to departments that request special projects?

13. Are procedures for hiring outside consultants implemented where appropriate?

TRANSACTION PROCESSING SERVICES

In the traditional financial services and internal control role, controllership objectives focus on maintaining effective transaction processing systems. Controllers ensure that these systems process information effectively and with adequate controls to safeguard assets. In this role, controllers typically have responsibility for the functions defined in the following section.

Effective transaction systems result from adequate segregation of responsibilities in functional departments and from consistent treatment of activities that affect financial information. An effectiveness review of transaction processing services should consider:

- General accounting
- Purchasing and accounts payable
- Personnel and payroll
- Order entry, billing, and accounts receivable

- Cash management
- Fixed asset management

Policies and procedures for general accounting and subsidiary systems should describe the full scope of activities performed by these departments, including error detection and correction. Departments should segregate approval and processing duties to minimize opportunities to mismanage assets. Accounting practices should be consistent with generally accepted accounting principles. Reporting should provide management with timely and accurate information in sufficient detail to evaluate performance and manage the business.

General Accounting

Evaluation of the general accounting function should consider the processes for:

- Summarizing and recording all financial transactions affecting an organization
- Summarizing and reporting the impact of actual financial transactions on operations and financial position
- Reporting actual versus budgeted financial transactions
- Performing key tasks related to proper control of cash receipts and bank account reconciliation

Evaluating the general accounting function should consider the following areas:

- Categorization of data (chart of accounts)
- Data accumulation and storage
- Journal entry processing

- Interfaces with subsidiary systems
- Closing procedures
- Reporting
- Cash control
- Bank account reconciliation
- Accounting controls

Purchasing and Accounts Payable

Evaluation of purchasing and accounts payable activities should include analyses of invoice and check processing, general ledger interfaces and vendor inquiry. All systems that support this function should be examined for appropriate levels of controls.

The nature and extent of linkages with treasury, general accounting, and other financial information systems should also be examined for adequacy.

Evaluating the purchasing and accounts payable function should consider:

- Requisitioning
- Vendor selection and analysis
- Purchase order processing
- Receiving
- Reporting
- Vouchering
- Invoice processing
- Disbursements
- Reporting

Personnel and Payroll

Evaluating the personnel and payroll activities includes review of the administrative aspects of hiring, paying, evaluating, transferring, promoting, and terminating employees. Labor cost controls also should be examined when evaluating this functional area.

Evaluation of the personnel and payroll function should consider:

- Recruiting practices
- Job application processing
- Appointment, promotion, transfer, and termination procedures
- Job classification, performance evaluation, and compensation analysis
- Time and attendance reporting
- Payroll adjustment processing
- Payroll deductions, net pay calculations, and employer liability policies
- Payroll check production, distribution, and reconciliation
- General ledger interface
- Funds sufficiency validation procedures

Order Entry, Billing, and Accounts Receivable

Evaluating the order entry, billing, and accounts receivable activities should include all procedures and controls that relate to product orders from the time of order entry through collection of customer payments. Both automated and manual processes should be evaluated for accuracy and appropriateness. Linkages with the treasury and credit departments should be examined and communication flows evaluated.

Evaluation of the order entry, billing, and accounts receivable function should consider:

- Order creation, modification, release, and reporting
- Invoice and credit memorandum processing
- Billing reporting
- Customer master file maintenance procedures
- Sales posting and cash application
- Customer statement preparation
- Monitoring of delinquent and uncollectible accounts
- Management and control reporting

Cash Management

Evaluating cash management services should encompass procedures to control both cash inflows and outflows. Methods used in collecting and monitoring cash inflows, disbursing and controlling cash outflows, and controlling intercompany transactions and transfers should be reviewed for adequacy. Internal and external automated systems for supporting cash management at the level required by the organization's cash transactions volume should also be evaluated.

The cash management function must respond to the results of business operations, including sales, purchases, capital expenditures and cash investment. Bank services and relations should also be monitored as they may affect disbursement activity and control. Because of the operational nature of the cash management function and its reliance on the operations of the organization, an effective review must consider the constraints placed on cash management by other functional areas.

Evaluation of the cash management function should consider:

- Methods of cash collections
- Methods of cash disbursements
- Intercompany cash management and clearing control methods
- Cash management systems
- Cash flow forecasting methods
- Banking service and relations

Fixed Asset Management

Evaluating the fixed asset management activities should include review of all procedures and controls for fixed asset acquisition, movement and transfer, adjustment and retirement. Manual and automated systems should be evaluated wherever they impact accuracy of records, tax data, or other management data (e.g., asset book value, insurance, and replacement cost data). Linkages with general accounts, financial planning, and tax and project accounting should be evaluated to ensure appropriate information flows. Approval and control procedures for movement or retirement of fixed assets should also be covered when evaluating this function.

Evaluation of the fixed asset management function should consider:

- Acquisition procedures
- Property control
- Accounting and tax analysis

- Retirements
- Reporting

TRANSACTION PROCESSING ATTRIBUTES

General Accounting

1. Is there a logically structured account code to define:
   a. Major accounts?
   b. Minor accounts?
   c. Budget area?
   d. Product?
   e. Cost center?
   f. Profit center?

2. Is the account classification easily recognized through a systematic numbering scheme?

3. Do major and minor account classifications exist that correspond to financial statements?

4. Is it possible to modify (and control modification of) chart of account codes and titles?

5. Is a chart of accounts dictionary periodically prepared and reviewed, including account:
   a. Number?
   b. Name?
   c. Status (active, inactive, restricted, etc.)?

6. Can the following current year data be retrieved for all accounts:
   a. Beginning balance?
   b. Detailed transactions by month (including source and type)?
   c. Month-end and year-to-date balances?

7. Can the following prior year data be retrieved for all accounts:
   a. Beginning balance?
   b. Total transactions by month?
   c. Month-end and year-to-date balances?

8. Can the following budget data be retrieved at meaningful detail and summary levels:
   a. Beginning balance?
   b. Budgeted amounts by month?
   c. Month-end and year-to-date balances?

9. Are all changes to prior year actual and current year budgeted amounts properly authorized?

10. Are statistical/operational data related to financial and operating performance maintained?

11. Does a listing of all changes to the financial data base (other than through normal transaction processing), showing before and after amounts and the source/reason for adjustment, exist?

12. Are all journal entries (including entries from subsidiary systems) edited prior to posting for:
    a. Balance (debits equal credits)?
    b. Valid account numbers?

13. Are all rejected entries, including reason for rejection, reported?

14. Have procedures been established to ensure proper processing of recurring standard journal entries (including entries from subsidiary systems)?

15. Is a monthly report produced that shows any recurring entries not made or made more than once?

16. Is the following information stored for each journal entry:
    a. Journal entry number?
    b. Entry date?

    c. Entry source (e.g., sales journal, purchase journal)?
    d. Transaction type (e.g., standard entry, reversing entry)?
    e. Debit and credit, account numbers, and amounts?
    f. Description/reason for entry?

17. Is the supporting documentation for each journal entry filed?

18. Are all journal entries throughout the period posted?

19. Can current period journal entries be processed without closing the prior period?

20. Are all journal entries reviewed and authorized?

21. Is special authorization required for journal entries:
    a. Affecting specified restricted accounts?
    b. Over specified dollar limits?

22. Does the general ledger system accept automated summary input from relevant subsidiary systems:
    a. Sales?
    b. Billing and accounts receivable?
    c. Payroll?
    d. Purchasing and accounts payable?
    e. Fixed assets?
    f. Inventory?
    g. Other?

23. Are edit and control procedures in place for entries from subsidiary systems to the general ledger?

24. Are reconciliations of general ledger and subsidiary ledger balances prepared on a monthly basis?

25. Does a monthly closing timetable exist, such as:
    a. First week after month end:
        Close all subsidiary ledgers?
        Summarize and post subsidiary ledgers to general ledger?
        Prepare and post all standard, accrual, and other closing journal entries?

Reverse previous month's accrual entries?
Prepare preliminary trial balance and other required listings/analyses?
b. Second week:
Prepare monthly financial reports?
c. Third week:
Reconcile all bank accounts?
d. Fourth week:
Begin cutoff procedures and subsidiary ledger closings?

26. Are the following reports produced on a timely basis:
a. Final trial balance?
b. General ledger detail and summary?
c. Account analyses for selected accounts?
d. Transaction analyses for selected transactions/sources?

27. Are the following reports prepared:
a. Balance sheet, including prior year balances for comparable period?
b. Income statement, including current period and year-to-date amounts for current and prior year?
c. Statement of cash flows, including current period and year-to-date amounts for current and prior year?

28. Are budgeted versus actual reports prepared, including the following data:
a. Current period?
b. Year-to-date?
c. Prior year?

29. Is the responsibility for budget control and financial reports assigned to the appropriate responsibility levels?

30. Are monthly reconciliations prepared for all bank accounts?

31. Is there an adequate, but not excessive, number of bank accounts to provide cash control by function, purpose, or location?

32. Is accurate and timely information regarding cash disbursements, receipts, and transfers provided?

33. Are cash receipts listed, restrictively endorsed and deposited daily?

34. Is there an adequate segregation of duties, including:
    a. Bank reconciliations versus cash receiving and disbursement?
    b. Cash receiving versus accounts receivable?

35. Are the accounting methods used consistent with generally accepted accounting principles for the industry/type of business?

36. Are the forms used to initiate and document all journal entries and file adjustments understandable?

37. Do general accounting principles and procedures manuals exist?

38. Are all policies and procedures manuals periodically reviewed and updated?

39. Is there an adequate number of staff with the proper level of experience and training?

Purchasing and Accounts Payable

1. Are requisition forms prenumbered?

2. Have inventory management policies and procedures such as economic order quantities, lead times, and minimum reorder point been established?

3. Is an inventory control system in place?

4. Are standardized inventory classifications used?

5. Is the stock list updated on a regular basis?

6. Are "rush" or emergency orders kept to a minimum?

7. Are requisitions processed on a timely basis?

8. Are bidding policies and procedures competitive?

9. Are vendors reviewed for authenticity and approved by appropriate individuals?

10. Is control over vendor file additions and deletions centralized?

11. Are periodic reviews of vendor files performed?

12. Do accounts payable and purchasing have a common vendor master file?

13. Do cross-references exist between parent companies and subsidiaries in the vendor file?

14. Is historical information on vendor orders, payments, pricing, and performance maintained and analyzed?

15. Are reports on vendor performance prepared and analyzed on a regular basis?

16. Are purchase orders prenumbered?

17. Are all purchase orders cut at the time of order?

18. Has a dollar limit been established, above which purchase orders must be utilized?

19. Has a price file for purchased items and priced purchase orders been established?

20. Have formal procedures been established to handle vendor inquiries efficiently?

21. Are purchasing transactions analyzed on a regular basis?

22. Have policies and procedures been established and forms been developed to count, inspect, and record items at the receiving point?

23. Is the receiving function independent of the purchasing function?

24. Are items in the receiving report agreed to the respective purchase orders at the time of receipt?

25. Are formal overage/shortage/damage reports prepared on a regular basis?

26. Are purchase commitment reports prepared on a regular basis?

27. Is there a logical interface between purchases, inventory, and the general ledger?

28. Are vouchers and invoice registers numerically controlled?

29. Are the data from purchase order/receiving/invoice automatically matched?

30. Are procedures in place for exception processing?

31. Are procedures to prevent processing of invoice copies in place?

32. Are debit memos utilized?

33. Have procedures related to vendor discounts been established?

34. Are account distributions coded and reviewed by knowledgeable parties?

35. Are invoices approved prior to payment in accordance with established procedures?

36. Is an effective voucher package and report filing system in place?

37. Are invoice payments monitored in accordance with established procedures?

38. Are check-signing, check-mailing, and voucher approval duties adequately segregated?

39. Is the use of manual (handwritten) checks limited to emergency situations?

40. Is the check stock adequately controlled?
41. Is a check-signing machine utilized for a substantial number of checks?
42. Is a countersignature required for checks over a certain dollar amount?
43. Is a check register produced for all checks generated?
44. Are supporting documents physically cancelled upon check signing?
45. Have procedures been established to prevent duplicate payments?
46. Are check-voiding procedures in place?
47. Are budget variance analyses prepared on a regular basis?
48. Is an aged trial balance prepared on a regular basis?
49. Have timely processing and standardized cutoff procedures been established?
50. Are control procedures in place for timely reconciliation of the aged trial balance with the general ledger reports?
51. Are adequate steps taken to investigate and eliminate recurring errors?

Personnel and Payroll

1. Have formalized management goals and objectives for recruitment been established?
2. Have near, intermediate, and long-term strategic planning for manpower needs been performed?
3. Are policies and procedures governing recruitment practices formally documented and updated on a regular basis?

4. Do the recruitment practices permit timely identification of potential candidates for vacant positions?

5. Are all applications screened against selected criteria to identify the most promising applicants to be interviewed?

6. Are prior employment and reference checks on candidates for employment completed on a timely basis?

7. Are guidelines and techniques for conducting interviews with and evaluating candidates for employment in effect?

8. Are applicants interviewed by the manager/supervisor for whom they will work?

9. Are controls in place to ensure that job positions are allocated and authorized before they are filled?
   Reports
   List of allocated positions
   List of authorized positions
   List of filled and vacant positions

10. Are controls in place to ensure that employees filling positions are eligible for those positions?

11. Are policies, procedures, and systems that permit employees to hold multiple job positions documented and followed?

12. Are policies and procedures for obtaining, selecting from, and purging employment registers formally documented and updated on a regular basis?

13. Can employment registers be obtained in a reasonable time frame?

14. Are employment registers updated as new applicants are approved for appointment or applicants are appointed from the registers?
    Report
    Employment registers by job classification/position and most recent date of update

15. Are policies and procedures governing appointments, promotions, transfers, and terminations, which are consistent with manpower goals and objectives, formally documented and updated on a regular basis?

16. Is there a formal appeal process for employees with grievances?
Report
    Appeal status and/or disposition and reasons

17. Are procedures for collecting and processing employee data formally documented?

18. Are the personnel and payroll data integrated to permit compliance with federal and state regulations?
Reports
    EEO records
    Labor statistics

19. Does a separate payroll/personnel group exist for collection and processing of:
    a. Appointments, promotions, transfers, and separations?
    b. Wage/salary rate and other adjustments?
    c. Withholdings and deductions?

20. Are the following employee data easily maintained?
Reports
    Turnaround personnel action forms
    All changes to employee data, detailing "before and after" change, effective date of change, and date of change submitted
    Employee history of:
        Appointments, promotions, transfers, and terminations by date
        Salary adjustments by date
        Ratings by date
        Education, skills, and job preferences

21. Is the access to and backup of employee data secured?
    Reports
    Inquiry transactions
    Backup files

22. Are required personnel actions promptly reported to the payroll and personnel group?
    Report
    Personnel actions due (e.g., performance rating, job audit)

23. Is the description of each job's eligibility requirements, responsibilities and duties, and salary ranges formally documented?

24. Are job classifications periodically reviewed for continued applicability?

25. Are job audits periodically performed to determine whether employees are performing duties above or below the requirements of their classification?

26. Is individualized attention given to an employee's abilities, job preference, and self-defined career goals?

27. Are promotion practices objective in identification, evaluation, and selection of candidates for positions?

28. Are controls in place to ensure that compensation guidelines are equitably applied across organizational units for similar job classifications?

29. Do the following personnel and payroll transaction validations exist:
    a. Position is allocated, authorized, and vacant?
    b. Pay rate falls within allowable range for job classification?
    c. Correct basis is used for calculating gross pay (hour, day, job function)?
    d. Correct basis is used for calculating deductions (percentage of gross, fixed amount)?

e. Employee is eligible for benefits?
f. Leave type is valid?
g. Employee is eligible for leave?
h. Leave balance is ≥ amount taken?
i. Employee is eligible for overtime and OT rate?
j. Labor distribution codes are valid?
k. Total hours reported is ≥ available pay period hours?

Reports
Transactions failing validity checks with intelligible reasons for rejection
Update control that identifies batches out of balance and rejected transactions, and lists all updates during the processing cycle

30. Is error correction processed within each payroll cycle?

Report
List of rejected transactions by date

31. Are suspended transactions revalidated completely?

32. Are policies and procedures for reporting employee time and attendance information formally documented and updated on a regular basis, including:
a. Hours worked by type?
b. Leave accrual rates and eligibility by type of leave?
c. Leave use?
d. Leave cash-in and reinstatement?
e. Leave balances allowed?
f. Overtime and shift differential eligibility?
g. Holiday pay eligibility?

33. Are methods for collection of labor information efficient, such as hours worked by product or workstation?

34. Is positive time input required for employees not working a standard number of hours?

Reports
Employees whose total hours reported are not $\geq$ available hours in pay period

Employees reporting nonstandard hours for which they were ineligible

Hours worked by type and employee for pay period, accounting period, quarter-to-date (QTD) and year-to-date (YTD)

Hours worked by labor distribution account

35. Is a report of leave use prepared for all employees?

Report
Leave taken/transferred/cashed-in by type, employee, and labor distribution account for pay period, accounting period, QTD and YTD

36. Are reports prepared of multiple types of pay, pay rates, hours, shifts, labor distribution, and leave per employee during the same pay period?

37. Is responsibility for preparation and approval of time and attendance documents segregated from documentation, coding, and processing functions?

38. Are controls in place to determine that total units upon which incentive compensation is based agree with total units actually worked?

39. Are policies and procedures governing payroll adjustments formally documented and updated on a regular basis?

40. Can the system make the following payroll adjustments:
    a. Gross and net pay adjustments?
    b. Withholding and deductions adjustments?
    c. Hours worked adjustments?
    d. Leave accumulation and used adjustments?
    e. Labor accounting distributions and accounting periods?
    f. Check cancellations/manual checks?

Report
List of all adjustments processed by employee

41. Can the system process payroll positive and negative adjustments as a part of regular payroll processing?

42. Are adjustments prepared and approved by the payroll and personnel group?

43. Do hour and dollar amount adjustments appropriately affect:
    a. General ledger balances?
    b. Prior pay, accounting, QTD, fiscal YTD, and calendar YTD periods?
    c. Vendor check amounts?

44. Is it possible to process manual checks and adjust all relevant payroll data after check issuance?

45. Are earnings accumulated by type on a pay period, accounting period, QTD, and fiscal YTD basis?
    Report
    Earnings by type, employee, and organizational unit on a pay period, accounting period, QTD, and fiscal YTD basis

46. Can the system calculate gross pay using shift differential wage rates and hours worked by shift?

47. Does the system perform the following for employees holding multiple positions:
    a. Combine for tax and other withholding calculations and for W-2 generations?
    b. Correctly distribute to labor accounts?

48. Are policies and procedures formally documented and updated on a regular basis for:
    a. Authorizing employee payroll deductions?
    b. Withholding deduction amounts according to a predetermined priority sequence?
    c. Refunding/collecting over/under withholding amounts?

89

49. Is there an adequate range of deduction types to meet the needs of employees, including:
   a. Federal income tax (FIT)?
   b. State income tax (SIT)?
   c. City/county income tax (CIT)?
   d. Federal Insurance Contributions Act tax (FICA)?
   e. Federal unemployment insurance (FUI)?
   f. State unemployment insurance (SUI)?
   g. State disability insurance (SDI)?
   h. Life and health insurance?
   i. Federal tax levies?
   j. Garnishments and child support payments?
   k. Deferred compensation?
   l. Credit union?
   m. Union dues?
   n. Other voluntary deductions?

50. Are controls in place to prevent the following:
   a. Total deductions from exceeding gross pay?
   b. Tax withholdings from exceeding the maximums?

51. Does the system include pay allowances and in-kind wages in the calculation of tax withholding amounts?

52. Are controls in place to ensure that payroll advances are recognized as reductions of net pay?

53. Are tax calculation methods promptly updated for changes in tax laws for multiple taxing entities?

54. Does the system calculate employer's liabilities each pay period for:
   a. FICA?
   b. Retirement?
   c. FUI?
   d. SUI?
   e. SDI?
   f. Workmen's compensation?

Reports
Checks to vendors for employee liabilities
Accrued employer's liabilities by vendor on a pay pe-
riod, accounting period, QTD, and fiscal YTD basis.
Amount of employee compensation by job classifica-
tion for workmen's compensation

55. Are employer's liabilities projected?

Report
Projections of employer's liabilities amounts by type

56. Are the employer's liability payments consistent with sound
cash management practices?

57. Is a periodic review of fringe benefit plans performed to
determine the most cost-effective options, including:
a. Competitive rates and benefits of carriers?
b. Employee co-pay options?
c. Benefit levels?

58. Are check stubs produced, detailing pay period and YTD:
a. Gross pay amounts by type?
b. Deduction amounts by type?
c. Net pay amount?
d. Expense reimbursement amounts?
e. Leave accumulated, used, and balance?

59. Are controls in place over the production and distribution
of checks, including:
a. Checks are prenumbered and stored in a secured environment?
b. Unusual check amounts are verified?
c. Check distribution is made by employees who do not
participate in any other payroll function?

Reports
Check register by check number, employee, organization unit, and check type (regular, handwritten, void, direct deposit)
Over/under check limit exceptions

60. Is the responsibility for payroll bank account reconciliations segregated from other payroll functions?

61. Are controls in place to ensure that payroll expenses are properly distributed to general ledger accounts?

Reports
Payroll amounts by account on a pay period, accounting period, QTD, and fiscal YTD basis

62. Does an audit trail of payroll entries to the general ledger exist?

Report
Detailed payroll transactions to general ledger

63. Do payroll transactions posted to the general ledger meet detailed financial reporting requirements of the organization?

64. Does the system update general ledger accounts for the appropriate accounting periods?

65. Can the system distribute:
    a. Same pay period hours and dollars to different accounting periods?
    b. Payroll amounts for employees being paid from multiple accounts on a percentage basis, dollar basis, or both?
    c. Labor hours/units of work to general ledger statistical accounts?

    Reports
    Units of work by account on a pay period, accounting period, QTD, and fiscal YTD basis

66. Are the responsibilities for processing general ledger entries and records segregated from the responsibilities for payroll processing?

67. Are guidelines and criteria for processing and rejecting payroll transactions formally documented and updated on a regular basis?

68. Does the system distribute payroll costs and units of work performed to the cost accounting system to permit accurate costing of products and reconciling of labor costs reflected in the payroll and cost accounting systems?

69. Are policies and procedures for submitting and processing claims for job-related expenses formally documented and updated on a regular basis?

70. Can job-related expenses be reimbursed as a function of payroll processing, with job-related expense reimbursements included in net pay amounts, but not as a part of gross taxable pay?

71. Is there a formal approach to developing the skills of employees, including:
    a. Continuing education curriculum?
    b. "In-house" staff development curriculum?
    c. Incentives for pursuing college degree programs?

72. Is a history of training received, education, and positions held maintained?
    Report
    Employee's training, education, and job experience

Order Entry, Billing, and Accounts Receivable

1. Are there well-defined criteria for acceptance of sales orders?

2. Are sales order authorizations in accordance with established procedures?

3. Are appropriate control features in place for method of order placement (e.g., mail, phone, telex)?

4. Are orders approved for acceptance of credit risk and customer account balances monitored against established credit limits?

5. Are customers requiring credit review flagged and placed in a pending file until the review is completed?

6. Are procedures in place surrounding the initiation and posting of blanket orders?

7. Are order data (customer number, inventory item number(s), salesperson number) validated at the point of order preparation/entry?

8. Are customer numbers controlled and assigned by the credit department?

9. Can both stocked and nonstocked inventory items be processed?

10. Is there strict control over use of price overrides?

11. Are rejected order data maintained for subsequent analysis and reprocessing?

12. Are strict controls in place over preinvoicing customers?

13. Are policies followed for matching inventory to the backorder file?

14. Has a policy regarding minimum order quantities and/or dollars been established?

15. Are backorder file inquiries made at the order entry point?

16. Are completed orders purged to an order/contract history file?

17. Are packing lists prepared and controlled?

18. Are orders released only after proper authorization?

19. Are the following reports prepared:
    a. Packing lists (multiple parts for billing, shipment acknowledgment, packing slip)?
    b. Open orders?
    c. Orders on hold?
    d. Orders for future shipment?
    e. Backordered items?
    f. Exception reporting of orders with nonstandard prices or manual price overrides?
    g. Exception reporting of customers exceeding credit limit?
    h. Order entry edits (invalid customer numbers, inventory numbers, etc.)?
    i. Contract status?
    j. Clerical productivity (for high volume systems)?
    k. Shipping bills of lading and labels?

20. Does the system initiate billing transactions for contracts billed on a regular basis?

21. Is a customer's accounts receivable balance for verification of credit limit status easily accessible?

22. Is a customer master listing for customer name, ship-to address, bill-to address, phone number, and so forth, easily accessible?

23. Is it possible to inquire into inventory files to determine inventory location, quantity on-hand, quantity committed?

24. Is order information forwarded to the materials planning/production scheduling systems?

25. Is order information forwarded to the marketing information system?

26. Are billing activities segregated from shipping and accounts receivable functions?

27. Are customer invoices prepared from properly approved orders and shipping documents?

28. Are invoices numerically controlled?

29. Are invoices priced from authorized price lists and according to authorized terms?

30. Are invoices reviewed by someone other than the invoice preparer for prices, terms, freight, other charges, and clerical accuracy?

31. Is the invoice edit register reviewed and are necessary corrections made?

32. Are reports of open orders, backorders and orders on hold monitored on a daily basis to identify when orders are shipped and should be invoiced?

33. Is there strict adherence to established approval procedures for credit memoranda?

34. Are all credit memoranda accounted for numerically?

35. Are credit memoranda for returned merchandise supported by authorized receiving reports?

36. Are credit memoranda for allowances supported by authorized customer service documents?

37. Are credit memoranda properly recorded in the sales returns and allowances account?

38. Are credit memoranda for returns and allowances forwarded to accounts receivable for proper customer credit?

39. Are credit memoranda control totals balanced to the manual calculations of credits?

40. Are the following statements prepared and utilized:
    a. Transaction and edit reports?
    b. General ledger sales journal?
    c. Sales tax report?

d. Discount summary?

e. Price override report?

41. Are the cost of goods sold and inventory journal entries posted to the general ledger?

42. Is fulfilled order information forwarded to sales analysis for sales analysis reporting?

43. Are there an established credit policy and procedures requiring credit investigation and approval and establishment of customer credit limit prior to adding a new customer to the master file?

44. Is there centralized control of customer master file maintenance to ensure that all authorized (and only authorized) file changes are processed?

45. Are all maintenance transactions recorded in a transaction file?

46. Have procedures been established for handling negative customer balances?

47. Are the invoice preparation duties segregated from accounts receivable posting?

48. Are authorized credit/debit memoranda for sales returns, sales allowances, and billing error corrections posted to customer accounts?

49. Are all invoice and credit/debit memo numbers accounted for to ensure authorized use and proper recording?

50. Is extensive transaction editing performed for valid transaction numbers, customer numbers, dates, and amounts?

51. Have suspense processing procedures been established?

52. Are accounts receivable control totals compared to billing control totals to ensure proper recording of invoices and billing adjustments?

53. Is there an audit trail of all transactions posted to customer accounts?

54. Are cash receipts processing and payment adjustment authorization segregated from accounts receivable recording?

55. Are cash receipts control totals from cash receipts forwarded to accounts receivable?

56. Are procedures in place for identification and review of payments that do not match an invoice amount?

57. Are payment transaction types separately identified?

58. Are payment amounts verified to identify unearned discounts, unauthorized deductions, and over- and underpayments?

59. Are chargebacks for unearned discounts, unauthorized deductions and over- and underpayments posted to customer accounts?

60. Is extensive transaction editing required for valid transactions, customer numbers, dates, and amounts?

61. Are accounts receivable control totals compared to cash receipts control totals to ensure proper recording of payments?

62. Is there an audit trail of all payment transactions posted to customer accounts, highlighting unapplied payment amounts and chargebacks?

63. Are accounts receivable transaction records physically protected?

64. Is the statement preparation function segregated from the statement review and mailing function?

65. Has a policy been established regarding customer statement generation (e.g., all customers, selected customers, only delinquent accounts)?

66. Are customer statements generated with account transaction detail and total payment due?

67 Has a policy been established that details delinquent account follow-up and collection procedures and the write-off approval process?

68. Is responsibility for initiation of proposed write-offs segregated from write-off approval authority?

69. Are approved write-offs of accounts deemed uncollectible properly posted?

70. Is there an audit trail that details account write-offs?

71. Are the following reports prepared and utilized:
    a. Transactions registers (including edit and batch control reports, suspense listing, cash and noncash registers, purge reports)?
    b. Transaction listing for a specific customer, account, or invoice?
    c. Accounts receivable exception reports for customer credit limit exceeded, partial or unapplied payments, overdue accounts, unauthorized discounts, negative customer balance?
    d. Accounts receivable trial balance?
    e. Aged accounts receivable detail and summary reports?
    f. Special accounts receivable significant status report by requested parameters (e.g., "over 90 days and $5,000")?
    g. Customer account history?
    h. Inactive customer accounts listing?
    i. Cash forecast (based on current receivables)?
    j. Customer listing?

72. Are the accounts receivable recording responsibilities segregated from general ledger balancing and posting functions?

73. Are journal entries for accounts receivable charges, credits, collections and write-offs (including freight charges, sales tax, discounts, sales returns, and allowances) summarized?

74. Is a reconciliation of the accounts receivable trial balance and the general ledger balance performed on a timely basis?

Cash Management

1. Are cash collection and disbursement methods listed and analyzed?
2. Are systems, collection, and bank delays identified?
3. Are total float delays (nos. 2–4) identified, monitored, and regularly reviewed for each cash collection method?
4. Are internal processing costs identified, monitored, and regularly reviewed for each cash collection method?
5. Have limits of authority been established for approval of cash disbursements?
6. If a formalized netting system is used for intercompany payments:
   a. Is the netting system managed from a centralized location?
   b. Can subsidiaries have investment balances *and* netting system deficits at the same time?
   c. Is there a date for zero balancing?
   d. Are target balances set?
   e. Has a detailed review been undertaken to ensure that the procedures relating to intercompany transactions have been rationalized so that transit time in the movement of funds is kept to a minimum?
7. If a formalized pooling system is used:
   a. Is concentration banking used regionally/worldwide for pool management?
   b. Is regular evaluation undertaken of the costs/benefits of pooling versus external investment/financing?
   c. Are accumulation accounts used?

8. If automated cash management systems (Citicash, Chem-link) are utilized:
   a. Are the following balance monitoring and account analysis reports used:
      Worldwide cleared balances and histories?
      Previous and current day debit and credit statements?
      Lock box and target balances?
      Balance controls?
   b. Are the following position reports used:
      Netting center balances?
      Marketing center balances?
      Pooling center balances?
   c. Are movement of funds reports used for:
      U.S. dollar transfers?
      Depository transfer checks?
   d. Are marketing information reports used for:
      Interest rates?
      Foreign exchange rates?
      Market activity?
      Hedging advice?

9. Are policies and procedures surrounding cash collections and disbursements formally documented?

10. If counterparty services are reviewed on a regular basis:
    a. Are counterparty yields compared?
    b. Are costs (interest and fees) compared?
    c. Are margin/spreads on foreign exchange deals compared?
    d. Are there regular meetings to discuss whether effective use is being made of available banking services?

11. Are counterparty limits regularly reviewed and are counterparty limits set for:
    a. Local banks?
    b. International banks?
    c. Investments?

d. Foreign exchange transactions?

e. Hedge transactions?

12. Can the number of bank accounts be rationalized?

13. Do authority limits exist?

14. Are check payments and bank transfers made in accordance with security and controls procedures, that is:
    a. Signing authorities/mandates?
    b. Control of check-signing machine?
    c. Security of unissued checks?

15. Are there procedures that are formally controlled, particularly with respect to:
    a. Preparation, issue, and amendment of instructions to bankers?
    b. The approval of authorized signatories?
    c. Delegation of authority and authority limits?

16. Is there an effective reporting system for bank balances on a daily and monthly basis?

17. Does the company enjoy good relations with their central bank, monetary authorities, and other financial institutions?

18. Are there practices in debtors management that can result in reduction of float time?

19. Are the organization's credit terms critically reviewed at regular intervals with marketing personnel?

20. Have there been any significant trends in the debtors aging compared with previous periods, after discounting seasonal factors?

21. Do the present follow-up ("dunning") procedures with respect to the organization's credit control operation ensure that:
    a. The dunning procedures are instigated as soon as possible after the due date for payment has passed?

    b. The procedures do not encourage customers to take advantage of the broad categories used in the age analyses?

    c. Customers compute their credit terms from the invoice date rather than the statement date?

    d. The due date for payment is clearly indicated on all invoices?

    e. Credit limits are established for all customer accounts?

    f. The general terms of business are rigorously enforced?

22. Have direct debiting opportunities been evaluated?

23. Are there practices in creditors management that can result in an increase of payable float (reverse float)? (This is the maximum delay between payment being initiated and the relevant account losing use of funds.)

24. Have there been any significant trends in the creditors aging compared with previous periods, after discounting seasonal factors?

25. Do the organization's payment procedures ensure that:

    a. Liabilities are only settled after taking the maximum advantage within the constraints laid down?

    b. Invoices are systematically scheduled to ensure that payment is only initiated at the expiration of a given credit term (and not before)?

    c. Payment mechanisms are determined by reference to reverse float opportunities?

    d. Competitive quotations are obtained for disbursements made in foreign currencies?

26. Are there practices of stock control that can reduce excess investment in stocks of raw materials, work in progress, and finished goods?

27. Have there been any significant trends in stock levels compared with previous periods?

28. Are poor earners identified?

29. From flowcharts of the production process, are there any delay points or storage pools at any locations?

30. Can larger input batches be used to take advantage of higher purchase discounts?

31. Can customers hold higher stock levels with reduction in the company's inventory levels of finished goods?

32. Do requests for purchases come from authorized personnel?

33. Is purchasing undertaken as competitively as possible?

34. Are stock levels quickly highlighted when they either exceed the planned maximum or fail short of the planned minimum?

35. Are treasury and sales departments involved in regular review of maximum/minimum reorder levels for product/material stocks?

Fixed Asset Management

1. Are capital acquisitions processed from accounts payable and/or project accounting systems for direct purchases or completed CWIP?

2. Are leases properly classified as capital or operating in accordance with FAS 13?

3. Are lease classifications justified prior to acquisition?

4. Are capital transactions readily traceable to feeder systems and source documents?

5. Are transactions strictly monitored and audited to ensure propriety of capital treatment?

6. Are policies and procedures in place to govern capital treatment, including:
   a. Capitalized overhead for CWIP?

b. Capitalized interest costs for CWIP (re: FAS 14)?

c. Capitalized adjustments?

d. Capitalized repairs?

e. Capital costs incident to purchases (e.g., sales tax, transportation, installation costs)?

f. Reasonable cutoffs on smaller items (e.g., all items < $500 expensed)?

g. Classification criteria for capital/operating leases (re: FAS 13)?

7. Is the approach used for capitalization consistently applied (e.g., like assets handled similarly)?

8. Are capital purchases subject to the same controls for purchasing, receiving, and invoice processing as other noncapital purchases?

9. Is investment tax credit (ITC) automatically calculated for qualifying acquisitions?

10. Do the asset records include the following elements for property identification:
    a. Division/department?
    b. Location/plant/building?
    c. Unique control number?
    d. Description?
    e. Manufacturer/model/serial number?
    f. CWIP number (or PO number)?
    g. Responsible individual?
    h. Owner (leases)?
    i. Contract number (leases)?

11. Are unique control numbers securely affixed to assets where practicable (includes most plant and equipment items)?

12. Are asset movements routinely identified and recorded via standardized forms that require proper approval from transferring and receiving departments?

13. Are periodic physical inventories taken via:
    a. Statistical sampling?
    b. Dollar exposure (emphasizing high dollar items)?
    c. Total physical?

14. Are discrepancies from physical counts communicated for accounting adjustments?

15. Are periodic audits taken of deeds, titles, and lease contracts to certify ownership (or nonownership)?

16. Are specific safeguard and requisition procedures in place for highly valuable assets (e.g., gold, silver) and easily movable equipment or paperwork (e.g., tools, deeds)?

17. Is access to assets permitted only in accordance with management authorization?

18. Are policies and procedures in place to govern asset movements, physical inventories, audits of deeds, titles and contracts, and general custody of assets?

19. Do the asset records include the following insurance valuation identifiers:
    a. Original costs?
    b. Percentage for physical depreciation?
    c. Insurance value?
    d. Industry code?

20. Are periodic insurance appraisals taken to assess adequacy of insurance coverage?

21. Are appraisal records traceable to fixed asset records?

22. Are policies and procedures in place for insurance needs and considerations?

23. Are maintenance and repair expenses recorded from feeder systems, providing the following types of information:
    a. Current period and life-to-date expenses?
    b. Times serviced?

    c. Date of last service?
    d. Vendor/contract number/expiration date?
    e. Preventive or emergency?

24. Is equipment needing regular maintenance identified and are schedules established?

25. Are maintenance budgets established in the appropriate functional departments?

26. Are the utilization and productivity of assets reviewed?

27. Are idle assets identified and alternative uses (including sale) considered?

28. Are the costs of repair and technological advances considered in reviewing the status of major equipment and facilities?

29. Do the asset records include the following elements for accounting and tax analysis:
    a. Division/department?
    b. Asset class?
    c. Product class?
    d. Useful life (book and tax)?
    e. Salvage value (book and tax)?
    f. Acquisition date and method?
    g. General ledger account?
    h. Depreciation method(s) (book and tax)?
    i. ACRS recovery class/treatment?
    j. ITC class/treatment?
    k. New/used code?
    l. 1245/1250 code?
    m. Realty/personalty code?
    n. Tax jurisdiction code (state, city, district, county)?

30. In addition, do the lease records include the following elements for accounting and tax analysis:
    a. Operating/capital?

    b. Useful life?

    c. Imputed interest rate?

    d. Executory costs?

    e. Fair market value?

    f. Present value?

    g. Leasehold improvement?

31. Are assets carried at cost less appropriate provision for depreciation?

32. Are capitalized leases carried at present value of minimum lease payments (less executory costs) less appropriate amortization?

33. Do the depreciation calculations utilize current optimal methods and conventions, including:

    a. ACRS (straight-line)?

    b. ACRS (percentage rates)?

    c. Class life/ADR:

        Group?

        Item?

        Combined (group and item)?

    d. Straight-line unrecovered cost?

    e. Straight-line gross?

    f. Double-declining balance (2.00, 1.50, 1.25) with automatic switch to straight-line?

    g. Sum-of-the-years'-digits gross?

    h. Units of production?

    i. Unitary methods (state mandated)?

    j. Half-year convention?

    k. Modified half-year convention?

34. Are periodic reviews made to determine appropriate depreciation methods and assumptions in light of current economics (e.g., component vs. composite, salvage values, fair values of property)?

35. Are definitive policies and procedures in place to govern the depreciation method and assumption selection for fixed assets (including leased) for both book and tax purposes?

36. Is tax depreciation provided by the following categories:
    a. Individual asset and method?
    b. ADR class (group, item, or combined)?
    c. ACRS class (percentage rates or straight-line)?
    d. Tax jurisdiction?

37. Is book depreciation provided by the following categories:
    a. Individual asset and method?
    b. Asset class?
    c. Division/department?
    d. Product class?

38. Are intangible assets amortized and treated as noncurrent?

39. Are operating leases treated as period expenses?

40. Are assets held for sale written down to realizable amounts, as appropriate?

41. Are assets held outside the United States converted to dollars, as appropriate (re: FAS 52)?

42. Are the following types of tax analyses and calculations made:
    a. *ITC Allowable*—For qualifying acquisitions, new or used?
    b. *ITC Recapture*—For retirements on which ITC was initially taken? Difference between original ITC and actual computed? Adjustments made to actual?
    c. *Gain/Loss*—For retirements on both book and tax basis? Current total depreciation brought up to date and net value compared to proceeds, if any? Primarily by scrapping and abandonments (no proceeds), and sales and exchanges? I.R.C. Sections 1245, 1250, and 1231 provisions considered?
    d. *State/Local Asset Apportionment*—Assets apportioned in

accordance with state/local tax codes for use in determining state/local income tax?

43. Are the following types of analyses and calculations made for other regulatory requirements:
   a. *Replacement Cost*—Asset revalued using replacement cost indices (vary depending on industry) (SEC S-X)?
   b. *Cost/Reserve activity summaries*—Reconciliation of all balance sheet asset activity for time period (10-K, SEC S-X)?
   c. *Inflation Adjusted*—Assets revalued to current cost using current cost/contant dollar techniques (FAS 33, Financial Reporting and Changing Prices)?
   d. *Leases*—In addition to lease classification and valuation for balance sheet purposes, capital leases are categorized by property class and schedule of payments with minimum and contingent amounts (FAS 13, Accounting for Leases)?

44. Are book and tax journal entries made to the general ledger at least on a monthly basis for:
   a. Additions?
   b. Corrections?
   c. Movements?
   d. Retirements?
   e. Gains/losses (book and tax)?
   f. Depreciation (book and tax)?
   g. Amortization (book and tax)?
   h. Reserves (book and tax) ITC?

45. Are reconciliations performed monthly for general ledger entries and book and tax differences?

46. Is financial statement footnote information obtained routinely for significant asset commitments, procedural changes, or write-downs?

47. Is journal entry control over assets limited to key accounting personnel?

48. Are dispositions of fixed assets through sales, exchanges, scrappings, abandonments, and donations accurately and promptly recorded, and is an adequate history maintained?

49. Do the standardized forms and the flow of the forms ensure proper approvals over shipment, billing, and recording of retirement activity (controls similar to those of inventory)?

50. Are gain/loss calculations provided for book and tax purposes?

51. Does the tax calculation include I.R.C. Sections 1245, 1250, and 1231, provision summarizations?

52. Is the ITC recapture calculation automatically provided?

53. Are partial asset write-offs available within the system?

54. Are policies and procedures in place to govern retirement approvals and methods, gain/loss and ITC recapture calculations, and partial write-offs?

55. Are erroneous retirements reinstated with minimal clerical efforts?

56. Are assets held for sale reviewed for write-downs to realizable values?

57. Are applicable write-downs properly communicated to the record-keeping area?

58. Are fixed asset reports generated and distributed in a timely manner?

59. Are period and summary reporting provided at an account, class, and division/department level for additions, adjustments, movements, and retirements, with corresponding reserve and depreciation balances?

60. Is tax reporting provided in the following areas:
    a. ITC capture at acquisition (support for IRS Form 3468)?

    b. ITC recapture at retirement (IRS Form 4255)?

    c. Gain/loss at retirement (IRS Schedule D and Forms 4796 and 4797)?

    d. Annual tax depreciation (IRS Form 4562)?

    e. State apportionment of assets?

    f. Annual tax depreciation (state)?

    g. Real and personal property taxes?

    h. Assets by tax jurisdiction?

    i. Tax depreciation forecasts (quarterly)?

    j. Tax ledgers?

61. Is regulatory reporting provided in the following areas:

    a. Replacement cost (SEC S-X)?

    b. Inflation adjusted (FAS 33)?

    c. Cost/reserve activity summaries (SEC S-X, 10-K)?

    d. Leased assets (FAS 13)?

62. Is internal management reporting provided in the following areas:

    a. Insurance valuation?

    b. Inventory listings and movements?

    c. Maintenance and repair expenses?

    d. Leasing activity and valuations?

    e. Product class?

    f. Productivity?

    g. Book ledger?

    h. Book depreciation forecasts?

    i. Transaction and edit?

63. Does adequate segregation of duties exist in general accounting, tax, project accounting, purchasing, payables and receiving areas to prevent fraud, theft, or other misappropriation of company assets?

64. Are all transactions in accordance with generally accepted accounting principles (GAAP)?

TRANSACTION PROCESSING PERFORMANCE INDICATORS

General Accounting

1. Ratio of correcting journal entries for wrong account coding to total journal entries for a typical month.

2. Total number of hours spent in a typical month preparing financial reports.

3. Total number of new accounts added in a typical month.

4. Current number of inactive accounts.

5. Total hours spent preparing account/transaction analyses in a typical month.

6. Total number of complaints or requests to relate actual financial and operational results to established goals.

7. Ratio of correcting entries to total journal entries for a typical month.

8. Ratio of entries posted to invalid or inactive accounts to total journal entries in a typical month.

9. Total hours spent posting routine journal entries in a typical month.

10. Total hours spent correcting posting errors in a typical month.

11. Average number of journal entries on posting backlog over the past 12 months.

12. Average time lag between the initiation of a transaction and time of processing.

13. Total hours spent reconciling general ledger and subsidiary ledger balances in a typical month.

14. Number of unreconciled differences between general ledger

and subsidiary ledger balances for the month as a percentage of the average for the past 12 months.

15. Ratio of correcting/adjusting entries to total journal entries in the general ledger control accounts in a typical month.

16. Total number of working days required to close the accounts and prepare reports in a typical month.

17. Average number of overtime hours per accounting staff during closing in a typical month.

18. Total number of adjusting entries required in a typical month.

19. Length of year-end audit.

20. Total audit fees.

21. Number of complaints received at prior year-end that financial reports were not timely, accurate, and/or relevant.

22. Total variances between actual and budgeted year-end sales, net sales, gross margin, and net income as a percentage of the applicable budgeted amounts.

23. Average time lag between period-end and analyses of budget variances.

24. Average unreconciled difference between cash balances per books and cash balances per banks for the past 12 months as a percentage of the average booked cash.

25. Ratio of correcting/adjusting journal entries to total journal entries for the cash accounts in a typical month.

26. Average dollar value of correcting journal entries to cash over the past 12 months as a percentage of the average cash balance.

27. Total number of checks returned due to insufficient funds over the past 12 months.

28. Total hours spent reconciling cash accounts in a typical month.

29. Total qualified/disclaimed audit opinions received due to:

    a. Improper accounting methods

    b. Insufficient documentation of transactions

30. Total cases of fraud/embezzlement due to:
    a. Lack of segregation of duties
    b. Lack of proper transaction approval process

31. Average hours of training time per new employee.

32. Turnover of accounting department personnel in relation to total department over the past 12 months.

33. Highest total number of overtime hours worked for an individual in the accounting department over the past 12 months.

34. Number of times per year that policies and procedures manuals are reviewed and updated.

Purchasing and Accounts Payable

1. Total requisitions rejected from purchasing due to:
    a. Improper coding
    b. Unauthorized approvals in a typical month

2. Ratio of reorders to total orders for the past 12 months.

3. Ratio of rush orders/stockouts to total orders for the past 12 months.

4. Average backlog of unprocessed requisitions for the past 12 months.

5. Average hours spent on research per vendor.

6. Total number of duplicate vendors on vendor file.

7. Total number of inactive vendors on vendor file.

8. Total purchase orders prepared in a typical month.

9. Total purchases made without purchase orders in the past 12 months.

10. Average variance between purchase order amount and vendor invoice amount.

11. Ratio of unpriced purchase orders to total purchase orders over the past 12 months.

12. Ratio of confirming purchase orders issued to total purchase orders issued in the past 12 months.

13. Number of purchases on which discounts were not negotiated as a percentage of total purchases for the past 12 months.

14. Total hours spent handling vendor inquiries in a typical month.

15. Total number of receipts that are not supported by formal receiving reports in a typical month.

16. Average time lag in offloading goods due to improper customs documentation.

17. Total inventory shrinkage at physical inventory date.

18. Ratio of write-offs to total inventory at period-end.

19. Total number of insurance claims filed in the past 12 months.

20. Total value of damages, returns, or shortages not collected as a percentage of total receipts for the past 12 months.

21. Total number of missed delivery dates in the past 12 months.

22. Average monthly variance between inventory control and general ledger totals for the past 12 months as a percentage of the average month-end general ledger inventory balance.

23. Average monthly variance between physical and perpetual inventory records for the past 12 months as a percentage of the average month-end general ledger inventory balance.

24. Average time lag between receipt of invoice in accounts payable department and vouchering of the invoice.

25. Total invoices paid for which supporting documentation was

not available as a percentage of total invoices paid in the past 12 months.

26. Total checks returned or credit memos received for duplicate payments in the past 12 months.

27. Total number of unpaid invoices on backlog in a typical month.

28. Total dollar amount of vendor discounts that were available, but not taken, in the past 12 months.

29. Total number of invoices rejected by the system due to inaccurate account code distribution in a typical month.

30. Average time lag between request for report or voucher package and actual receipt of the requested item.

31. Average time lag between request for payment and actual disbursement as a result of misplaced check attachments.

32. Total number of manual checks used as a percentage of total checks issued in a typical month.

33. Total number of manually signed checks as a percentage of total checks signed in a typical month.

34. Total number of checks not requiring approval as a percentage of total checks issued in the past 12 months.

35. Total number of checks which were returned as duplicate payments in the past 12 months.

36. Total number of checks voided in a typical month.

37. Average monthly unreconciled difference between the aged trial balance and the general ledger over the past 12 months as a percentage of the average general ledger balance.

38. Total number of processing errors in a typical month.

39. Average time lag in reprocessing suspense file items.

Personnel and Payroll

1. Average time lag between authorization of a position and the time the position is filled.

2. Average hours of training for each employee involved in recruiting.

3. Average hours processing applications for a job opening.

4. Average hours spent per candidate making reference checks.

5. Amount by which actual labor costs exceed those budgeted as a percentage of total budgeted labor costs for the past 12 months.

6. Total hours spent reviewing and updating policies and procedures for appointments, terminations, promotions, and transfers per year.

7. Ratio of rejected transactions to total transactions for employee payroll and personnel data in a typical 12 months.

8. Total hours spent by payroll and personnel group employees making mass changes to employee records in a typical month.

9. Current number of inactive status records in the employee master file.

10. Total number of payroll adjustments made in a typical month.

11. Average time lag between identification of a required personnel action and the completion of that action.

12. Total number of job positions for which up-to-date, written descriptions of eligibility requirements, responsibilities and duties, and salary ranges are not available.

13. Total number of employee grievances concerning promotional opportunities, salaries, job assignments and duties in the past 12 months.

14. Employee turnover in the past 12 months.

15. Average yearly absenteeism per employee.

16. Average time lag in processing payroll due to late submittal of data, improper sequencing of transaction processing, or cumbersome error correction procedures.

17. Total number of handwritten payroll checks issued in a typical month.

18. Total number of rejected transactions as a percentage of total employee payroll and personnel transactions in a typical month.

19. Total hours spent each year reviewing and updating policies and procedures for reporting time and attendance.

20. Total hours spent collecting time and attendance data in a typical pay period.

21. Total number of reconciling items required to accurately reflect general ledger payroll distributions in a typical pay period.

22. Total hours spent reviewing and updating policies and procedures for processing payroll adjustments each year.

23. Total number of payroll adjustment errors as a percentage of total payroll adjustments processed in a typical month.

24. Amount by which withholdings exceed payroll deduction maximums for the past 12 months.

25. Total adjustments made to correct employee withholding amounts in a typical month.

26. Total manual checks issued in the past 12 months to account for deductions or withholdings that the system did not accommodate.

27. Average number of days in advance that employer's liability payments were made in the past 12 months.

28. Frequency with which the fringe benefit plan(s) is reevaluated.

29. Average time lag between generation and issuance of payroll checks.

30. Average time lag between the cancellation of an incorrect paycheck and the reissuance of a corrected paycheck.

31. Total number of employee inquiries regarding pay amounts and deductions in a typical month.

32. Total number of hours spent reconciling payroll reports in a typical month.

33. Amount of variance between payroll expenditures (and related statistics, if applicable), labor cost per the payroll reports and labor cost per the general ledger in a typical month.

34. Total amount by which payroll expenditures exceeded budgeted/allocated amounts or available funds in the past 12 months as a percentage of total budgeted expenditures.

35. Total number of hours spent reviewing and updating policies and procedures for updating general ledger records with payroll information per year.

36. Total hours spent identifying and analyzing causes of variances between actual and projected labor costs in a typical month.

37. Total hours spent each year reviewing and updating policies and procedures for claiming and reimbursement of job-related expenses.

38 Employee turnover rate for past 12 months.

39. Total number of positions that were filled by promotions within the firm in the past 12 months.

40. Total number of positions that were filled by outside hires due to lack of appropriate employees for promotion to the position in the past 12 months.

Order Entry, Billing, and Accounts Receivable

1. Ratio of total errors in item types, quantities, salesperson number(s), and so forth, to total orders processed in a typical month.

2. Total hours spent processing new customer orders in a typical month.

3. Total orders for which special pricing is used as a percentage of total orders placed in a typical month.

4. Average time lag between the rejection of an order and its resubmission.

5. Average time lag for a backorder to be filled once inventory becomes available.

6. Total number of items on back order.

7. Total number of open orders on file.

8. Total number of emergency or rush orders processed as a percentage of total orders in a typical month.

9. Average number of items in the credit pending file over the past 12 months.

10. Total number of items which were preinvoiced as a percentage of total invoices in the past 12 months.

11. Total number of customer complaints regarding order item errors or orders not filled on a timely basis received in a typical month.

12. Ratio of rejected shipments to total shipments in a typical month.

13. Total hours spent preparing packing lists in a typical month.

14. Total orders reported for which there were no bills of lading or labels as a percentage of total orders in a typical month.

15. Average time lag between initiation of an order, receipt of customer data, and commencement of order processing.

16. Amount of book-to-physical inventory adjustment required after the last physical inventory was taken as a percentage of the book inventory balance.

17. Average time lag between the calculation of sales commission and application.

18. Frequency with which the marketing department is updated on orders received or order status.

19. Total number of customer complaints regarding disagreements with invoices received in a typical month.

20. Total number of hours spent correcting the invoice edit register in a typical month.

21. Total number of credit memoranda processed in a typical month.

22. Total number of hours spent preparing required sales tax reports in a typical reporting period.

23. Total dollar amount of trade discounts allowed as a percentage of total sales in a typical month.

24. Total items for which price overrides are allowed as a percentage of total items invoiced in a typical month.

25. Total errors generated in the billing/general ledger interface in a typical month.

26. Total number of the following in a typical month:
    a. Additions to the customer master file
    b. Deletions from the customer master file
    c. Changes to the customer master file

27. Total number of hours spent maintaining the customer master file in a typical month.

28. Total active customers on the customer master file.

29. Total inactive customers on the customer master file.

30. Total number of sales transactions in a typical month.

31. Total dollar sales volume in a:
    a. Typical month
    b. Peak month

32. Total hours spent balancing billing control totals to control totals from invoices posted to customer accounts in a typical month.

33. Average time lag between identification of a suspense transaction and correction of the transaction.

24. Total number of hours spent on suspense processing in a typical month.

35. Total dollar amount of unmatched credit/debit memoranda as a percentage of sales volume in a typical month.

36. Total number of customer complaints regarding inaccurate invoice amounts on customer statements received in a typical month.

37. Total remittances processed in a typical month.

38. Dollar amount of discounts or deductions taken by customers upon payment as a percentage of total sales in a typical month.

39. Total hours spent correcting edit reports in a typical month.

40. Percentage of cash receipts posted to customer accounts:
    a. Within one day of receipt
    b. Within two days of receipt
    c. After two days of receipt

41. Total number of remittances that are suspended due to lack of supporting documentation in a typical month.

42. Total customer complaints regarding payment discrepancies received in a typical month.

43. Total hours spent reconciling closed invoice items to payments received or credit memoranda in a typical month.

44. Total customer complaints regarding errors on customer statements received in a typical month.

45. Average time lag between customer inquiries regarding account balances, open items, payments received, and so forth, and the company's response.

46. Average number of customer discrepancies reconciled on backlog over the past 12 months.

47. Total number of accounts with outstanding balances under $100.

48. What percentage of the average accounts receivable balance is:
    a. Less than 30 days past due?
    b. 31–60 days past due?
    c. 61–90 days past due?
    d. 91–120 days past due?
    e. Over 120 days past due?

49. Total hours spent following up delinquent accounts in a typical month.

50. Total write-offs of accounts deemed uncollectible as a percentage of total sales for the past 12 months.

51. Total hours reconciling accounts receivable subsidiary ledgers to the general ledger in a typical month.

52. Average unreconciled difference between the accounts receivable subsidiary ledgers and the general ledger as a percentage of the average total general ledger balance over the past 12 months.

53. Total budget variances resulting from inaccurate account code distributions as a percentage of the total sales per the general ledger in a typical month.

Cash Management

1. Total cash receipts in a typical month.

2. Percentage of cash receipts over the past 12 months in the following form:
   a. Checks
   b. Bank transfers
   c. Direct debits
   d. Cash
   e. Other

3. Average time lag between completion of sales transaction and invoicing of the customer.

4. Average time lag between receipt of check and deposit to the bank.

5. Average time lag between invoicing of customer and receipt of payment.

6. Average internal processing cost for each of the following collection methods:
   a. Checks
   b. Bank transfers
   c. Direct debits
   d. Cash
   e. Other

7. Total cash disbursements in a typical month.

8. Percentage of cash disbursements over the past 12 months in the following form:
   a. Checks
   b. Bank transfers
   c. Direct debits
   d. Cash
   e. Other

9. Average time lag between completion of a purchasing transaction and receipt of the invoice from the vendor.

10. Average internal processing cost for each of the following disbursement methods:
    a. Checks
    b. Bank transfers
    c. Direct debits
    d. Cash
    e. Other

11. Average transit time per transaction for the movement of funds in a formalized netting system (if present).

12. Number of transactions made through use of automated cash management systems in a typical month.

13. Frequency with which policies and procedures for cash collections and disbursements are reviewed and updated.

14. Frequency with which counterparty services are reviewed.

15. Frequency with which counterparty limits are reviewed.

16. Total number of bank accounts.

17. Total number of hours spent reconciling bank accounts in a typical month.

18. Average unreconciled difference between the bank and the general ledger cash balances as a percentage of the average general ledger cash balance over the past 12 months.

19. Percentage of the average accounts receivable balance:
    a. Less than 30 days past due
    b. 31–60 days past due
    c. 61–90 days past due
    d. 91–120 days past due
    e. Over 120 days past due

20. Days past due point at which collection efforts are initiated.

21. Total interest collected on overdue accounts in the past 12 months.

22. Total dollar amount of invoices paid more than 2 days before the due date over the past 12 months.

23. Average number of competitive quotations obtained prior to making a disbursement in a foreign currency.

24. Fluctuation amount in stock levels from the prior to current year.

25. Frequency with which stock lines are reviewed for poor earners.

26. Total purchase discounts taken in the past 12 months.

27. Total purchase discounts available, but not utilized, in the past 12 months.

28. Average time lag between a stock level exceeding its planned maximum and correcting action.

29. Average time lag between a stock level falling short of its planned minimum and correcting action.

30. Frequency with which maximum/minimum reorder levels for product/material stocks are reviewed by the treasury and sales departments.

Fixed Asset Management

1. Dollar amount above which items are capitalized; below which items are expensed.

2. Total acquisitions (dollar amount) in the past 12 months.

3. Total number of accounting errors in project accounting and accounts payable as a percentage of total transactions processed in a typical month.

4. Dollar limit above which capital acquisitions require special review.

5. Total number of hours spent reviewing these capital acquisitions in a typical month.

6. Frequency with which physical inventories are performed.

7. Variance between physical count and general ledger balance at the last physical date as a percentage of the general ledger balance.

8. Frequency with which audits of deeds, titles, and lease contracts are performed.

9. Frequency with which insurance appraisals are taken.

10. Total cost of preventative maintenance per year.

11. Average downtime per year to perform equipment repairs.

12. Variance between budgeted and actual repair and maintenance expense as a percentage of the total budgeted expense for the past 12 months.

13. Average lead time allowed in requests for major asset acquisitions.

14. Total hours spent preparing book and tax depreciation analyses in a typical month.

15. Frequency with which assets held for sale are reviewed for write-down to realizable values.

16. Total hours spent preparing general ledger and book and tax reconciliations in a typical month.

17. Average unreconciled difference between detailed fixed assets registers and the general ledger as a percentage of the average general ledger balance over the past 12 months.

18. Total hours spent reviewing and assessing fixed asset footnote information in a typical month.

19. Total clerical hours attributed to tax and regulatory requirements in a typical month.

20. Average time lag between retirement of an asset and reporting as such.

21. Average book gain/loss on asset retirements over the past 12 months.

22. Average variance between estimated useful life of an asset and age at which the asset was retired for retirements made in the past 12 months.

23. Total amount of ITC recapture in the past 12 months as a percentage of the total ITC originally taken on the retired assets.

24. Total number of hours spent reinstating book and tax data for erroneously retired assets in the past 12 months.

25. Frequency with which assets held for sale are reviewed for write-downs to realizable value.

26. Average time lag betwewen period-end and availability of key management information reports.

27. Total hours spent adjusting various book numbers for use in tax reports in a typical month.

28. Frequency with which fixed assets policies and procedures are reviewed and updated.

5

PERFORMANCE REPORTING

Managers need reliable information to evaluate performance and to plan and implement strategy. Accurate and timely performance reporting is basic to effective management control. Information systems structured by well-defined procedures and processes for recording and reporting transactions are the primary sources of management information.

An effectiveness review of performance reporting capabilities should consider:

- Information structure
- Information flow
- Management reporting
- External reporting

In many organizations, the chief financial officer traditionally has had responsibility for directing the growth of information systems. The financial function had primary responsibility to safeguard the organization's assets. It often had the greatest demands for financial and operational data. Based on management and external reporting needs, the financial function determined basic information structure and flow. Coupling these needs with the costs of establishing systems, the chief financial officer was a logical choice to control information system development.

As information systems are evolved to effectively meet the performance reporting and information needs of multiple, sophisticated users, the chief financial officer should continue to control information system development. He should understand the fundamental needs of other functional areas. Manufacturing needs include timely and accurate product cost information. Marketing requires information to support pricing decisions. Information essential to other functional areas may reside in systems whose information structure, flow, and reporting capabilities are dictated by the financial function.

Organizations increasingly use state-of-the-art information technologies and applications to establish competitive advantage. Since the chief financial officer has responsibility to assess and report the overall performance of the organization, he has a strong interest in ensuring the integrity of data generated by these information systems. By ensuring that necessary internal controls are in place, he enables management and key users to have reliance on information developed for financial reporting and management decision making.

INFORMATION STRUCTURE

Information structure defines how financial, operational, and statistical data are maintained in the information data bases. Organizations benefit from an information structure that supports multiple reporting requirements and formats. Management expects that information structure design has flexibility to support current and future reporting needs with minimal disruption of information flow to key users.

The objectives of evaluating information structure include determining that:

- Data classifications can support changing information and reporting requirements
- Information structure design permits summarization and consolidation at multiple levels

The account structure, defined by the chart of accounts, should be the basis for compiling all financial information. Account structure should be logical and sufficiently detailed to support collection, summarization, and reporting requirements. Organizations collect financial information by processing financial transactions. These transactions should conform to the established account structure. Account structure design should have flexibility to readily accept changes to the chart of accounts. It also should permit various methods of sorting and categorizing accounting detail for reporting purposes.

Many companies require multiple levels of consolidation reporting. Consolidation capabilities should automatically include allocations and eliminations of intercompany transactions. The information structure also should support multiple paths for consolidations such as legal entity, geographic location, product segment, and business group.

INFORMATION STRUCTURE ATTRIBUTES

1. Identify the measures used to monitor performance against strategic and operating plans:

a. Are performance measures established for all essential business activities? Identify any gaps.

b. Does each performance measure adequately present the status of the business activity it is intended to monitor?

2. Are industry standards, such as ratios and net sales statistics, used as key indicators in the current reporting system?

3. Identify and classify the key reports used at the corporate and functional/operating levels. Do these reports include:

a. Management reports comparing actual performance to key statistics, industry standards, budgets, and past performance?

b. Performance reports focusing on geographic area, significant lines of business, products, and so forth?

c. Special reports providing management with information to make decisions based on corporate strategy, industry standards, and other key indicators?

d. External reports satisfying requirements of stockholders, regulatory agencies, tax authorities, creditors, and other outside entities?

4. Identify information and reports that key users need but do not receive.

5. Identify information and reports that management receives but does not use.

6. Does report detail support the information needs of the intended user? For example, do exception reports used by operating managers provide sufficient detail to pinpoint specific problem areas requiring corrective action?

7. Does report content generally include:

a. Narrative describing information in the report?

b. Operating and financial data?

c. Year-to-date, current-month, and other summarizations?

    d. Highlights of key information followed by supporting detail?

8. Identify key information required by multiple users. Do key users receive this information in sufficient format, detail, and time frame to meet their needs?

9. Review the account structure used to classify financial data:
   a. Identify any inconsistencies between the current account structure and key information needs of management.
   b. Do all financial transactions conform with the existing account structure?

10. Are accounts maintained in sufficient detail:
    a. Do accounts effectively support collection, summarization, and reporting?
    b. Do transactions and subsequent reports supply sufficient detail to perform business analyses?

11. Identify key financial and statistical data maintained in information data bases:
    a. How frequently are these data updated?
    b. Does the frequency of these updates support management needs?

12. Does the hierarchy of the current account structure support data groupings and report requirements of management?

13. Evaluate the flexibility of the account structure:
    a. Can accounts be added easily? Deleted easily?
    b. Can account detail be sorted and characterized in multiple ways?
    c. Can reports be structured independently of the chart of accounts?
    d. Does account structure support multiple consolidations?
    e. Does the account structure provide sufficient detail for planning and decision support activities?

INFORMATION FLOW

Information flow describes how data are accepted and processed by the financial function using manual and computer-based methods. Managers must have confidence in the accuracy and reliability of management information. Information flow governed by well-defined procedures and controls ensures consistent processing of financial data and increases the accuracy and reliability of management information.

The objectives of evaluating information flow include assessing:

- Procedures for capturing data
- The integrity of data received and processed by the financial function

Organizations should have procedures that accurately describe the flow of financial information. Procedures for accumulating and processing data should identify all personnel responsible for providing and processing data and should describe the tasks each performs. Procedures should define the collection methods used. The level of automation used to process financial data should dictate the level of detail required to clearly describe procedures. For example, procedures for general ledger transactions posted through an automated interface from subsidiary systems could require less detail than procedures for a stand-alone system using manual entries.

Regardless of the level of automation, using manual and automated controls should maximize data quality from the financial function. Controls provide consistent processing of financial data. Adequate controls, by detecting inaccurate or improper transactions, should ensure that management receives accurate, reliable information. They should increase management confidence in data integrity by establishing the means to correct data errors. Controls for manual and computer-based systems should include adequate segregation of duties, detailed transaction identification, and control of total reconciliation for batched data. Controls for computer-based systems should include the use of special features, such as automated allocation, currency conversion, and consolidation capabilities.

INFORMATION FLOW ATTRIBUTES

1. Review the information flow for manual and computer-based systems including automated interfaces:
   a. Are control schedules used to ensure that data received by the financial function are processed consistently and accurately?
   b. Identify the manual and computer-based controls used in processing financial information.
   c. Are processing schedules clearly described to ensure that data are processed in the correct order and priority?

2. Review procedures for:
   a. Chart of accounts maintenance
   b. Data collection responsibilities
   c. Report format and content updates
   d. Data categorization
   e. Reconciliation between interfaces
   f. Retention
   g. Documentation updates

3. Evaluate procedures in the following ways:
   a. Do procedures accurately describe how these activities are performed?
   b. Do they identify the who, what, when, why, and how of these activities?
   c. Are procedures reviewed and updated on an established

schedule to ensure that they accurately reflect current practices?

4. What special skills or knowledge is required to access data in manual and automated systems?

5. What security measures are maintained to permit and restrict access to manual and computer-based systems, and do such measures include a schedule to periodically review access to these systems?

6. As information needs change, do procedures exist to receive, evaluate, and respond to user requests for additional information, reports, or processing capabilities?

   a. Do procedures include establishing priorities to user requests?

   b. Do procedures require user approval for changes to ensure that any modifications to the information flow are implemented correctly?

7. Does the organization have formalized controls and processes for developing and modifying automated systems? Describe the key features and limitations of these processes.

MANAGEMENT REPORTING

Effective management reporting provides the tools to plan, evaluate, and control operations and to ensure appropriate use and accountability of resources. Management reports should accurately reflect business operations and provide sufficient information for decision making.

The objectives of evaluating management reporting capabilities include assessing:

- The extent that management reporting meets information needs and supports decision making

- The types, quality, and timeliness of reports used by management to operate the business

Management reporting systems should support multiple users and maintain accounting control for accurate report content. Report formats should be consistent across an organization to enhance the reporting system's ability to meet a variety of needs. The information structure and flow that support the reporting system should be designed to recognize the specific information needs of different functional areas. Reporting requirements should be clearly defined for each functional area.

Reporting systems should include features to confirm data integrity and to control access to sensitive information. Financial data should be subject to appropriate accounting control. Access to financial data and reports should be restricted to authorized users. Internal and external reports should be reconciled regularly to ensure data integrity. Report accuracy should be evaluated in terms of the type, materiality, and frequency of errors and adjustments.

Management expects accurate and timely reports. Some functional areas will require daily reports while others require monthly reporting. Reporting periods generally should reflect fiscal and planning cycles and should provide sufficient time for management to act upon the information. Information type and detail required in management reports will vary by user.

Management reporting systems provide managers with performance reporting to determine company performance against key statistics and standards, responsibility reporting to assess how cost centers are performing, and exception reporting to highlight variances in key financial and operating statistics. Performance reporting should focus on significant segments of the business, such as product lines and geographic regions. It should include appropriate industry and competitor comparisons. The performance reporting system also should be linked to short-term and long-range planning information. Responsibility reporting should identify significant plan deviations for each responsible manager or functional unit. Exception reporting detail should be tailored to identify significant exceptions to enable management to focus corrective actions on those areas.

MANAGEMENT REPORTING ATTRIBUTES

1. Does the management reporting system support information requirements of multiple users, such as tax, treasury, and planning as well as the needs of nonfinancial users?

2. Do management reports use consistent reporting formats wherever applicable?

3. Is adequate accounting control exercised over management reports?
   a. Does accounting control include reconciliation between reports intended for internal and external use?
   b. Is all financial data under accounting control?

4. Does the information structure support management reporting requirements by providing:
   a. Adequate focus on all functional areas, but particularly for those that support essential business activities?
   b. Data structured to facilitate access by multiple users and at successive management levels?

5. Does information flow that supports management reporting include:
   a. An information hierarchy that tracks logically from the chart of accounts?
   b. Clearly defined and controlled report distribution?
   c. Standard input forms?
   d. One information flow into a central data base?

6. Evaluate report accuracy by determining the type, materiality, and frequency of most common errors and adjustments.

7. Are management reports prepared consistently within a fixed number of days after period end?

8. Evaluate the timeliness of management reporting:
   a. Do reporting periods generally match cycles of major business lines and activities? Planning cycles? Other cycles?
   b. Does the reporting system allow adequate time for action between report cycles?
   c. Are nonroutine report requests evaluated and completed promptly?
   d. Are reporting cycles adequate for functions and units that perform or support essential business activities?

9. Do and should management reports include features such as:
   a. Graphics to display trends and relative values?
   b. Narrative for additional comments?
   c. Comparison of current period results to prior periods?
   d. Summary of year-to-date performance?
   e. Inclusion of statistical or operational data?
   f. Comparisons with industry data?
   g. Highlights with supporting detail?

10. Does performance reporting provide:
    a. Comparisons against the industry and/or competitors?
    b. Information where applicable by business or product/service lines or geographic region?
    c. "Linkage" between long-range financial and management planning and short-term reporting?
    d. Adequate focus on all significant business activities?

11. Does responsibility reporting provide:

    a. Appropriate information detail to support intended management use at successive management levels?
    b. Sufficient detail to investigate significant deviations from plans?
    c. A format that encourages corrective action by highlighting negative results when they occur?

12. Does exception reporting:
    a. Highlight significant problems and deviations from planned results?
    b. Support tracking of identified exceptions?
    c. Clearly define the threshold for reportable exceptions?

13. Does exception reporting to top management include reports such as:
    a. Corporate financial and operating highlights?
    b. Key financial and operating company statistics?
    c. Consolidated balance sheet and income statement?
    d. Consolidated statement of changes in financial position?
    e. Financial and operating variances from planned results?
    f. Cash-flow statements?
    g. Significant trends?

14. Does exception reporting to division management include reporting such as:
    a. Division financial and operating highlights?
    b. Key financial and operating divisional statistics?
    c. Summaries of orders received, unfilled, and backlogged?
    d. Production statistics?

15. Does exception reporting to department management include reports such as:
    a. Department income and expenses compared to budget?
    b. Key production, sales, and operating statistics?
    c. Cost center summaries?
    d. Labor cost and efficiency?

e. Expense summaries?
f. Technical performance reports?

EXTERNAL REPORTING

All organizations prepare external reporting, whether as financial statement reporting to shareholders, tax reporting to the Internal Revenue Service, or regulatory reporting to governmental bodies, such as the Securities and Exchange Commission (SEC) or industry-specific agencies. Each external report may have a standard format representing a variation of internal reporting.

The objectives of evaluating external reporting capabilities include determining:

- Specific external reporting requirements
- The extent that existing reporting capabilities support multiple external reporting requirements

External reporting systems should have flexibility to respond to multiple users in terms of report content and filing requirements. Financial statement reporting to stockholders, creditors, and the SEC must be prepared in accordance with accepted accounting principles. Reporting should reflect the development and consistent application of accounting principles. It also should recognize the reporting requirements of outside auditors.

Tax and regulatory reports to governing agencies must conform to standards, content, and reporting requirements defined by those agencies. Companies must know and understand all of their regulatory reporting obligations including the reporting of deadlines, resource needs for report preparation, and penalties for improper or late filings.

EXTERNAL REPORTING ATTRIBUTES

1. Do external reporting capabilities meet the information requirements of tax, accounting, and regulatory authorities?
2. Do external reporting capabilities support different timing and filing requirements?
3. Do external reports use standard reporting formats whenever applicable?
4. Is adequate accounting control exercised over external reports?
   a. Does accounting control include reconciliation between various external and internal reports?
   b. Is all financial data under accounting control?
   c. Is access to financial data controlled?
5. Does the information structure support external reporting by providing:
   a. Adequate focus on all reporting areas?
   b. A data structure that includes appropriate cross-referencing when account structures differ for internal and external reporting?
6. Does information flow that supports management reporting include:
   a. An information hierarchy that tracks logically from the chart of accounts?
   b. Clearly defined report distribution?
   c. One information flow to a central data base?
   d. Ability to identify information for external reporting only?
7. Are external financial reports prepared in accordance with generally accepted accounting principles (GAAP)?
   a. Are outside auditors retained to render an opinion on financial statement compliance with GAAP?
   b. If financial statements do not conform with GAAP, what

significant adjustments are required to obtain conformance?

8. Evaluate regulatory reporting requirements:
   a. Are all regulatory requirements identified?
   b. Are filing requirements documented and understood?
   c. Are external experts consulted, as needed, on technical filing matters?
   d. Are technical reference services maintained to support filing investigations?
   e. Are regulatory authorities used as information resources where allowed?
   f. Are filings prepared correctly and submitted in a timely manner to avoid penalties for improper or late filings?

9. Evaluate tax reporting capabilities:
   a. Are tax policies and procedures documented?
   b. Are tax requirements understood for federal, state, and local tax authorities?
   c. Is reponsibility for monitoring income tax regulations clearly defined?
   d. Are tax filings prepared correctly and submitted in a timely manner to avoid penalties?

6

TREASURY

The effectiveness with which an organization obtains and manages cash resources profoundly influences the ways in which it operates. Organizations need effective treasury services to ensure that adequate cash resources are available when needed. Treasury activities rely on internal cash flow and external economic information, including interest rates, exchange rates, and economic forecasts. Treasury services strive to make cash available only when needed and to optimize all other cash through a strategy that balances future cash flow assumptions against the risks associated with lack of cash. This balance is achieved through cash investment, financing, and cash mobilization activities. An effectiveness review of treasury services should consider:

- Environment
- Cash management
- Cash flow forecasting

- Banking services and relations
- Currency and exposure management

Although not included as an area for review in this book, treasury services also include funds management activities for investing idle cash and financing operations to minimize interest expense.

Organizations unable to manage their cash resources operate at a disadvantage by having to devote significant management attention to seek and conserve funds. Ineffective treasury services may force management to forgo opportunities desirable to achieve strategic objectives. These opportunities could include expansion of current operations, acquisitions, or technology and capital improvements.

A review of treasury must consider the impact of internal organizational constraints and external environment factors on managing cash resources. For example, observing dispersed banking relationships does not necessarily recommend consolidating cash balances to make treasury services more efficient. Dispersing cash balances due to the availability and location of credit lines may have merit if such practices enable the organization to pursue opportunities that achieve strategic objectives.

ENVIRONMENT

The treasury environment defines the scope and level of treasury services. Evaluating the treasury environment considers the specific cash management needs of the organization including currently unmet needs. Management should know whether treasury activities reflect current practices and technologies and support strategic objectives. Understanding the treasury environment looks to the technical capabilities, organizational structure, and sophistications of treasury services.

The objectives of evaluating the treasury environment include determining the:

- Qualitative and quantitative goals of treasury and how those goals are met
- Mix of centralized and decentralized activity
- Relationships between treasury and other oganization units
- Functional reponsibilities of treasury
- Extent of treasury documentation
- Use of computer-based systems to support treasury activities
- Level and mix of transaction activity

Defining the treasury environment establishes guidelines for performing an effectiveness review. Identifying treasury goals and the means by which they are measured provides a basis to judge whether treasury services support the organization's overall objectives and are achieved effectively. Evaluating the mix of centralized and decentralized activities as well as the relationships between treasury and other organizational units should detect gaps between management expectations and the actual quality of treasury services. The evaluation should also indicate the degree of management support of treasury activities and the extent of cooperation by organizational units providing input and receiving output from treasury. Treasury documentation should delineate the organizational structure and control systems governing treasury activities. Understanding computer-based systems and transaction activities and volumes may indicate the complexity and sophistication of available treasury services. It also may point to areas requiring improvement or expansion of existing computer-based services.

TREASURY ENVIRONMENT ATTRIBUTES

1. Identify treasury's primary goals and objectives.

2. What specific measures and criteria are used to evaluate treasury performance?

3. Determine the extent and purpose of centralized and decentralized treasury activity for:
   a. Cash management
   b. Financing
   c. Investments
   d. Currency and exposure management

4. What are the scope and nature of significant treasury relationships with other organizational units, such as accounts payable, controller, or others?

5. Does treasury fulfill an advisory role to management? Define the advisory role and identify levels of management benefiting from this advisory process.

6. Do functional responsibilities for cash management include:
   a. Cash collections?
   b. Cash disbursements?
   c. Intercompany cash management?
   d. Cash management systems?

7. Do treasury responsibilities include cash flow forecasting?

8. Do treasury responsibilities for banking services and relations consider the scope and type of accounts required for operating needs?

9. Do responsibilities for currency and exposure management:
   a. Factor foreign and domestic political conditions?

    b. Incorporate appropriate hedging techniques?

    c. Conform with established procedures?

10. Do funds management activities consider short- and long-term financing and investments.

11. Are job descriptions for treasury services current and complete?

12. Do treasury policies and procedures accurately match the scope of treasury functions and activities?

13. Are key policy issues impacting treasury activities identified by management?

14. What banking and external systems support treasury activities?

15. What internal systems support treasury activities?

16. Are transaction levels, volumes, and fluctuations monitored for:

    a. Check disbursements?

    b. Deposits?

    c. Investment activities?

    d. Account transfers?

    e. Foreign exchange contracts?

    f. Debt instruments?

    g. Multiple banks and banking locations?

    h. Letters of credit?

    i. Intercompany receipts, payments, and transfers?

CASH MANAGEMENT

Cash management defines those daily operations that permit treasury to meet near-term cash requirements, particularly cash receipt and disbursement activity. It is highly interactive with banking systems and dependent on accurate cash flow forecasting. Effective cash management should enable an organization to conserve and mobilize cash resources when needed. It should control working capital and the physical movement of cash internally and externally. The objectives of evaluating cash management should include determining the adequacy of:

- Methods used to collect and monitor cash inflows
- Methods used to disburse and monitor cash outflows
- Controls to monitor intercompany cash transactions and transfers
- Internal and external automated systems to support cash management at the level and cash transactions volume required by the organization

Cash management should be responsive to the results of business operations, including sales, purchases, capital expenditures, and cash investment. Cash management effectiveness increases when coordination exists with other treasury services, such as cash flow forecasting. Cash flow forecasting and investment activities may impact decisions relating to cash collections. Effectively used banking services and well-maintained banking relations also may affect collections and disbursement activity and control.

CASH MANAGEMENT ATTRIBUTES

1. Do cash collection methods allow for:
   a. Cash?
   b. Checks?
   c. Bank transfers?
   d. Direct debits?
2. Are changes in collection patterns adequately identified and monitored?

3. Are cash collection delays tracked for:
   a. Mail time?
   b. Physical collection time?
   c. Check processing time?
   d. Float?

4. If cash collection delays are frequent, what are the primary reasons for these delays?

5. Are collection costs monitored for bank fees, as well as for internal costs?

6. Have cash collection alternatives been evaluated, such as manual lock boxes, and electronic funds transfers?

7. Is management satisfied with cash collection reporting and analysis? What are the identified shortcomings?

8. Can the credit approval process be improved?

9. Are procedures adequate for aged receivables collections?

10. Do cash disbursement methods allow for:
    a. Cash?
    b. Checks?
    c. Bank transfers?
    d. Direct debits?

11. Are changes in disbursement patterns adequately noted and monitored?

12. Is cash disbursement activity tracked for:
    a. Optimal timing from invoice receipt to disbursement?
    b. Physical collection time including mail and vendor processing?
    c. Float?

13. Does disbursement activity make use of cash discounts and allowances?

14. Is disbursement activity monitored and analyzed?

15. What disbursement aging methods are used?

16. Are disbursement processing costs analyzed, such as clerical costs and bank fees?

17. Are disbursement alternatives, such as direct debit instead of checks, adequately considered?

18. Is disbursement activity integrated with cash flow forecasts?

19. Is management satisfied with disbursement reporting and analyses? Identify any shortcomings.

20. Is appropriate responsibility established for managing intercompany transactions?

21. Are foreign currency requirements integrated between subsidiaries and parent company?

22. Are target cash balances set, monitored, and periodically reviewed?

23. What procedures and methods determine the currency used for intercompany payments?

24. What reconciliation methods track "due from" and "due to" transactions?

25. Are internal and bank cash concentration systems used?

26. Are internal and bank cash investment management systems used?

27. Are criteria adequate for selecting cash management systems and networks?

28. Are cost-benefit or other analyses used to support the selection of cash management systems?

CASH FLOW FORECASTING

Cash flow forecasting predicts daily operational cash requirements and activities. Forecasts are based on assumptions about the economic environment and business operations. Cash flow forecasting also evaluates forecasted against actual cash requirements to ensure that internal and external assumptions are realistic.

The objectives of evaluating cash flow forecasting include determining the effectiveness, adequacy, and sophistication of:

- Cash flow forecasting assumptions
- Cash flow support systems

Cash flow forecasting should operate together with cash and investment management services to meet daily cash transaction requirements.

CASH FLOW FORECASTING ATTRIBUTES

1. Are cash flow forecasts prepared at the parent, subsidiary, group, or other levels?
2. Where in the organization are cash flow forecasting assumptions determined?
3. Are cash flow forecasting assumptions and systems adequate with respect to:
   a. Horizon?
   b. Currency?
   c. Capital and operating budget integration?
   d. Matched and unmatched currencies?
   e. Investment and financing decisions?
   f. Automated systems capabilities?
4. Are cash flow forecasts tracked against actual cash needs?
5. What internal and external cash management systems support cash flow forecasting? Which of these systems, if any, depend on an external data base?

6. To what extent are cash flow forecasting systems integrated with formal accounting systems?
7. Is actual operating data used in forecasting systems available in a timely manner to support cash flow forecast updates?
8. Is management satisfied with the adequacy of current cash flow formulas and parameters?

BANKING SERVICES AND RELATIONS

Responsibilities for banking services and relations include establishing, controlling, and reporting bank accounts, services, and activities. Effective banking services and relations support other treasury activities including cash management, cash flow forecasting, and currency and exposure management. Management wants cost-effective and competitive banking services that may include bank accounts, networks of accounts, transfer mechanisms, investment vehicles, cash operation services, and balance reporting.

The objectives of evaluating banking services and relations should include determining that:

- The scope of bank accounts supports the operational and organizational needs of the organization
- Banking services are cost-effective
- Adequate controls exist for using bank services, including credit lines and account maintenance
- Proper levels of communication are maintained with the banking community
- Cash accounts are organized appropriately into a cash management function
- The investment of funds and the placement of cash balances meet the requirements of exposure management

Environmental factors including overall business objectives, the location of operations, and the needs of other treasury activities will shape banking services and relations. For example, a company with international operations will require banking relationships that provide international services, including networks, cash concentration, and clearing systems. Banking services also should include access to foreign currency markets and dealer operations, if otherwise unavailable.

BANKING SERVICES AND RELATIONS ATTRIBUTES

1. What are the scope and type of bank accounts, including:
   a. Number of accounts?
   b. Links to credit lines?
   c. Links with cash management systems?
2. Are bank services evaluated and selected on the basis of cost, availability, and effectiveness?
3. Do adequate controls exist for:
   a. Check payments and transfers?
   b. Instructions for bankers?
   c. Approval and changes of authorized signatures?
   d. Delegation of authorization limits?
   e. Account maintenance?
   f. Credit line establishment?
4. Is management satisfied with available daily and monthly balance reporting?
5. Are cash account balances adequate with respect to:
   a. Cash collection and disbursement requirements?
   b. Short-term investment policies?
   c. Compensating balance requirements?
   d. Credit lines?
   e. Operating requirements?

6. What methods determine services, such as foreign exchange and hedge transactions, required of large money center banks?

7. How is banking service effectiveness monitored?

8. What methods determine the services, such as payroll processing and check cashing, required by local banks?

9. What key reports support monitoring of bank activity?

10. Is management satisfied with the adequacy of reporting and analyses of bank services and relations? What are the identified shortcomings?

CURRENCY AND EXPOSURE MANAGEMENT

Currency and exposure management minimizes risks, such as loss of principal and interest, arising from domestic and foreign currency transactions and investment. Effectively managing currency and operations exposure protects the profitability of daily operations, particularly for companies with foreign operations. An effective currency and exposure management approach strives to balance daily liquidity requirements and investment and financial opportunities. Too cautious an approach may result in idle cash balances, while a poorly managed approach may produce unplanned interest expenses. Well-planned currency and exposure management optimizes the timing of cash needs, maximizes interest revenue from invested idle cash, and minimizes interest expenses.

The objectives of evaluating currency and exposure management should include determining that:

- Effective communication and control are maintained between the treasurer and organizational units responsible for planning and executing currency and foreign currency transactions

- Segregation of responsibility is well-defined, particularly for organizations with significant dealer operations
- Performance goals are defined and monitored
- Mechanisms exist to identify interest and currency exposure
- Foreign currency transaction requirements, generated independently from treasury but within the organization, are coordinated to optimize gains and losses from these transactions
- Effective external hedging techniques are used to manage interest rates and foreign currency transaction exposure

Currency and exposure management has potential to contribute to the overall profitability of an organization. Although not responsible for the origination of currency and exposure transactions, currency and exposure management contribution to profitability may be significant, depending on the total value of its cash balances and investment portfolio. As an operation, treasury should minimize the financial risk associated with meeting domestic and foreign currency requirements, while optimizing the return on invested cash.

A review of currency and exposure management should evaluate links to cash flow forecasting and investment management activities. Communication from cash flow forecasting and investment activities will impact the timing and effectiveness of currency and exposure management activity and performance.

CURRENCY AND EXPOSURE MANAGEMENT ATTRIBUTES

1. Is communication adequate and effective between treasury and other groups involved with foreign exchange transactions?

2. Do control procedures for credit limits and transaction amounts identify:
   a. Maximum total amount of individual spot foreign exchange deals that may be made with any individual institution?
   b. Maximum total amount and period of individual forward foreign exchange contracts that may be made with any individual institution?
   c. Maximum total amount and period of individual deposits or short-term borrowing that may be arranged for hedging?

3. Are individual operating responsibilities adequately separated by:
   a. Dealing function?
   b. Clerical and recording function?
   c. Accounting and reporting function?

4. Is the currency management function adequate for identifying, executing, recording, and reporting foreign exchange transactions?

5. Is currency management performance evaluated on the basis of:
   a. Efficiency of spot market measured?
   b. Effectiveness of cover measured?

6. Is exposure an important consideration to the organization? Consider the effect on:
   a. Cash flow, balance sheet, and profitability from an exchange rate shift
   b. Debt service from an interest rate shift

7. Does the exposure plan:
   a. Define limits for the extent that exposure may vary from zero by currency and by time?
   b. Include adequate monitoring procedures?

8. Do administrative and procedural requirements adequately define authority limits for hedging transactions?

9. Is foreign exchange exposure defined and measured for:
   a. Transaction exposure?
   b. Translation exposure?
   c. Economic or cash flow exposure?

10. Are internal hedging techniques, such as matching cash flows, netting, cash management, and pricing considerations used to manage foreign exchange exposure?

11. Are external hedging techniques, such as foreign contracts, currency options, financial futures, and investment-borrowing combinations used to manage foreign exchange exposure?

12. Are internal hedging techniques used to manage interest rate exposure?

13. Are external hedging techniques, such as financial futures and interest rate swaps, used to manage interest rate exposure?

14. Do exposure management activities:
   a. Identify unmatched cash flows?
   b. List available hedging options?
   c. Evaluate alternative hedging options?
   d. Record and report hedges?

15. Does exposure management consider tax and foreign exchange control consequences?

7

INTERNAL AUDIT

Organizations depend on an effective internal audit function as an essential managerial control. Linked but not restricted to the financial function, internal audit has a broad mission to ensure that adequate protection exists for an organization's assets. Internal audit fulfills this mission by evaluating systems and methods of internal control using financial and operational audits.

Management objectives and needs should define the scope of internal audit activities. Financial auditing focuses on evaluating and verifying the flow and accuracy of accounting information. Because key operational controls also must exist, internal audit services include auditing operational practices, systems, and controls. These audits extend beyond financial services into other functional areas, such as production, information services, and marketing. To the extent that an organization uses computer-based systems and controls, internal audit evaluates those systems as part of financial and operational reviews.

Results of these audits give management a better understanding of the adequacy of key controls and can provide detailed assessments of the:

- Accuracy and reliability of financial and operating information
- Levels of compliance to policies, procedures, and outside regulations
- Operational efficiencies of the systems under review

An effectiveness review of the internal audit function should focus on four key elements:

- Scope of internal audit activities
- Audit planning
- Audit performance
- Organizational independence

Focusing on these areas provides an evaluation of the internal audit function based on its organizational position and status. The evaluation can produce comparisons of actual internal audit performance against management expectations. It may highlight gaps between an organization's control systems and the technical expertise and resources available to evaluate them.

SCOPE OF INTERNAL AUDIT ACTIVITIES

Internal audit scope establishes the role played by the internal audit department in an organization. Scope delineates the responsibilities and purpose of internal audit activities. It tells an organization where auditing emphasis will be placed. Scope reflects underlying management commitment to internal audit studies and probable support for resulting findings and recommendations.

The objectives of evaluating the scope of internal audit activities include determining that:

- An approved policy statement describes the purpose, responsibilities, and source of authority for internal audit activities
- Activities emphasize evaluating control systems to ensure data integrity and to assess operational efficiencies
- The internal audit department reviews and tests computer-based systems and addresses broader data security issues
- Internal audit scope clearly defines responsibilities for verifying compliance to policies, procedures, and regulations
- The scope of operational audits is clearly defined and consistent with management objectives
- Internal audit access to upper management and the audit committee is explicitly stated

Organizations realistically define internal audit scope when staffing levels, depth, and technical expertise reasonably match the complexity of existing control systems. How effectively the internal audit department achieves stated objectives may signal that internal audit scope be redefined or staffing deficiencies corrected. In addition, the frequency and degree to which changes in audit activities occur should cause management to reassess expectations of internal audit's role within the organization.

Many organizations use the internal audit staff for special projects beyond previously established audit scope. Internal audit effectiveness may be impaired if these projects compete for staff or disrupt audit schedules. Since internal audit departments may draw from other financial and functional areas for staffing needs, objectivity may be compromised if auditors evaluate activities that they previously performed. Refer to the section on organizational independence later in this chapter for further discussion of these issues.

Organizations of all sizes use computers as part of their internal control systems. Internal audit scope should encompass computer-based systems when an organization relies on them to generate and store key financial and operational information. Internal audit staff evaluating computer-based systems should have sufficient technical knowledge of those systems. Audit scope should address data security, computer installation effectiveness, and disaster recovery planning. Scope should be broad enough to enable internal audit to recommend control improvements to computer-based systems prior to their installation.

SCOPE OF INTERNAL AUDIT ACTIVITIES ATTRIBUTES

1. Is a formal policy statement maintained for the internal audit function?
2. Does the internal audit policy statement describe:
   a. Purpose and objectives?
   b. Overall responsibility?
   c. Source of authority?
3. Do upper management and audit committee approve the internal audit policy statement? If not, where is approval obtained?
4. Is the internal audit policy statement consistent with management objectives, including strategic and business plans?
5. Is the policy statement periodically reviewed and revised?
6. Do internal audit activities include:
   a. Evaluating manual and computer-based control systems?
   b. Verifying operational efficiencies against budgets, busi-

ness and strategic plans, and other performance standards?

   c. Monitoring compliance to policies and procedures, industry guidelines, and regulations?

7. How are internal audit activities documented?

8. Do internal audit activities include financial and operational audits? Do audits include key computer-based systems?

9. Does internal audit have sufficient access to upper management and the audit committee? What is the quality and frequency of internal audit communication to those groups?

10. Is management responsive to internal audit findings and recommendations? Does operating management:
   a. Cooperate fully with internal audit activities?
   b. Complete corrective steps recommended by internal audit in a timely manner?

11. Is the internal audit function regarded as technically competent, objective, and comprehensive by:
   a. Upper management?
   b. Audit committee?
   c. Operating managers?
   d. Outside auditors?

AUDIT PLANNING

A comprehensive audit plan lays the foundation of an effective internal audit department. The audit plan documents management expectations of the internal audit function. It identifies specific studies to be performed in financial and operational areas. The plan assigns priorities to internal audit activities based on management needs and assessed risk. It identifies staffing levels to ensure effective completion of internal audit programs.

The objectives of evaluating internal audit planning include assessing:

- The appropriateness of criteria used to establish audit coverage
- Planning effectiveness for short-term and long-range planning horizons
- The risk factors to establish audit objectives and to write programs
- The extent of input and review by management and external auditors in the planning process
- The internal audit plan approval process
- The frequency, format, content, and distribution of audit results
- The extent of coordination between internal audit activities and external audit tasks

Audit planning requires a thorough understanding of an organization's internal controls. Internal audit should have criteria for assigning audit coverage based on the control system's complexity, data sensitivity, and history of associated problems. Risk factors used to establish audit priorities may be related to potential monetary losses, inadequately trained personnel, and transaction processing volumes. Audit planning of computer-based systems should consider risks related to data, physical site, and program security.

Successful audit plans incorporate reviews by management and external auditors to ensure management concurrence of audit priorities. Results of these reviews should be appropriately documented. The audit plan should be approved by the audit committee, senior management, or the board of directors prior to implementation. By ensuring that the plan reinforces overall management objectives, senior management and the audit committee establish detailed standards against which actual audit performance can be measured.

Long-range audit planning should consider effective staff utilization. The long-range audit plan should define required staffing levels for timely completion of activities. The plan should be integrated with the audit department budget and also should be coordinated with the scheduled activities of external auditors. Clearly documented, the long-range plan requires approval by the audit committee and senior management.

Audit planning requires flexibility to reassign resources as priorities shift and to report those changes to involved personnel. How audit progress is monitored and reported to management should also be assessed, as these changes should be followed by management approval.

AUDIT PLANNING ATTRIBUTES

1. Does audit coverage for organizational units and functions consider:
   a. Historical problems?
   b. Data sensitivity?
   c. Complexity of control systems?
   d. Transaction volumes?
   e. Staff turnover?
2. Are previous audit plans reviewed when establishing audit coverage?
3. Does operating management participate in establishing audit coverage?
4. Is the emphasis on financial, operational, and computer-based audits consistent with the scope of internal audit activities?

5. Is audit coverage for computer-based systems adequate to verify data, physical, and program security?

6. Do internal audit activities include review of information system designs?

7. Does internal audit perform information system control reviews?

8. Does the internal audit function include a long-range audit planning cycle?

9. Does the long-range planning cycle include adequate planning schedules and plan updates?

10. Is the internal audit long-range planning horizon consistent with the organization's planning horizons?

11. Does the long-range plan approval process include frequent and extensive reviews?

12. Does the long-range plan delineate staffing requirements?

13. Is the long-range plan integrated with internal audit department budgets?

14. Are procedures and systems in place to monitor internal audit progress against planned activities?

15. Are progress reports rendered frequently enough for timely detection of deviations from schedules and planned activities?

16. Are staffing levels and audit objectives reassessed as part of the progress reporting for internal audit programs?

17. Are material changes to audit plans communicated to the appropriate personnel?

18. Are internal audit programs coordinated with activities performed by outside auditors? Does this coordination include:
    a. Overlapping coverage of high risk areas?
    b. Coordination of report findings and recommendations?

19. Are internal audit schedules coordinated with operating management to consider:
   a. Production cycles?
   b. Financial reporting cycles?
   c. Systems design and implementation schedules?

AUDIT PERFORMANCE

Audit performance includes all aspects of executing the audit plan. Activities begin with developing detailed audit programs and conclude with reporting and follow-up on recommendations. Audit programs identify specific controls and tests to be evaluated and performed. Programs provide the outline for workpaper preparation and other documentation. Effective audit performance is measured by the efficiency demonstrated in executing the program. It is also based on the confidence that management and other key users place on the findings and reports.

The objectives of evaluating audit performance include determining that:

- Auditing fieldwork is conducted in a controlled, efficient manner with adequate staff supervision and review of results
- Testing and evaluations are documented and support conclusions and recommendations
- Actual performance is monitored against plan estimates to evaluate staff efficiencies and performance
- Management and external auditors place reliance on audit reports and workpapers

Effective audit performance results from compliance with established policies, procedures, and standards. Auditing policies should reflect accepted standards, such as those of the Institute of Internal Auditors, Inc. They should be comprehensive, clearly defined, and periodically reviewed and updated. Auditing policies should be consistent with overall corporate policies and integrated with more detailed departmental procedures. When necessary, procedures should be written using standard terminology and should be communicated to staff prior to conducting the audit program.

Audit programs should identify overall objectives, auditing issues, and risks. These programs should include resource estimates by area, task, and person. Audit budgets, actual performance statistics, and variance analyses should be used to evaluate audit effectiveness.

Workpaper documentation can indicate if activities were effectively supervised and if findings were sufficiently reviewed. This material should be logically organized so that persons not directly involved may review audit status and identify the basis of audit findings.

Effective reporting is the key communications tool of the internal audit department. Reports should document audit results and responses to audit findings. Although content may be dictated by report type, it should be consistent with industry standards and approved by management. Reports should be evaluated on clarity, conciseness, and completeness. The extent to which management and external auditors rely on these reports may indicate the quality and completeness of internal audit's work products.

An effective internal audit department should have procedures to monitor responses to report findings and to ensure timely follow-up by appropriate personnel. Procedures should state how responses will be structured to include pertinent information and should include criteria to assess the adequacy of those responses. Procedures should exist to evaluate and distribute replies and to complete required follow-up.

AUDIT PERFORMANCE ATTRIBUTES

1. Is audit fieldwork conducted efficiently with adequate supervision and review of results?
2. Are auditors briefed on special risks and the nature of key controls?
3. Do auditors review prior year audits and have access to sample records?
4. Are prior year audit findings used to identify areas for improvement and to document audit deficiencies?
5. Does the audit program include:
   a. Description of overall objectives?
   b. Assessment of issues?
   c. Budgets developed by task, area, and staff?
   d. Clearly defined tasks?
   e. Updates to address special conditions and scope changes?
6. Are budgets established for all audit programs?
7. Are audit personnel involved in developing budgets?
8. Are standard budget forms used?
9. Is time reporting sufficiently detailed to monitor actual results against budget?
10. Are budgets approved by management?
11. Are variance analyses used to explain deviations from budget?
12. Are prior year variances factored into the budgeting process?
13. Is workpaper documentation consistent from year to year?
14. Are internal audit documentation and standards consistent with:
    a. Corporate requirements?
    b. Industry standards?
    c. Professional standards?

15. Are internal audit reports consistent with industry and corporate standards with respect to:
    a. Content?
    b. Clarity?
    c. Support of findings by workpaper documentation?
16. Is audit report distribution:
    a. Approved by management?
    b. Controlled by established procedures?
17. Does audit report follow-up include steps for:
    a. Verifying assigned responsibilities?
    b. Logging and distributing audit responses?
    c. Auditing corrective activities performed in response to audit findings?

ORGANIZATIONAL INDEPENDENCE

An effective internal audit department must have organizational independence. Audit reports and findings are useful to management only to the extent that internal audit operates without interference from groups or individuals with potentially conflicting interests. Effectiveness increases when the audit function has direct and frequent access to the audit committee and senior management. Free access to information required to achieve stated objectives also increases internal audit effectiveness.

The objectives of evaluating the organizational independence of the internal audit function include determining that:

- Reporting relationships support the accomplishment of audit objectives
- Internal audit has access to all necessary records and resources

- Management and the audit committee have a commitment to internal audit activities indicated by the frequency and content of responses to reports
- Conflicts of interest are minimized

Reporting relationships with management and the audit committee should enable internal audit to achieve objectives without interference or diminished objectivity. Management commitment to internal audit independence is demonstrated by direct reporting of internal audit to a high-level financial officer or chief executive. The department preferably should not report directly to an operating executive with daily responsibility in other financial function areas, such as treasury or accounting.

Any special projects assigned to the internal audit department should be assessed for their impact on objectivity in performing future work. Projects requiring auditors to assume operating or design responsibilities should be noted; subsequent audits should be reviewed to ensure that auditors are not assigned to work that they previously performed.

ORGANIZATIONAL INDEPENDENCE ATTRIBUTES

1. Does internal audit have solid line reporting relationships to any of the following:
   a. Upper management?
   b. Board of directors?
   c. Audit committee?
2. Does internal audit have dotted-line reporting relationships to other organizational units? Identify those relationships.
3. Does the internal audit director have full responsibility for all internal audit activities?

4. Does management respond in a timely manner to implement internal audit recommendations?

5. Is the internal audit function centralized?

6. Do reporting relationships impact:
   a. Audit coverage?
   b. Staffing levels?
   c. Quality control?

7. Does the internal audit department have access to:
   a. Financial, operational, and personnel data?
   b. Organizational guidelines and procedures?
   c. Computer-based information systems?
   d. Internal correspondence and reports?

8. Is the internal audit department restricted from access to information? Describe that restricted information.

9. Does the internal audit staff perform special projects that could create future conflicts of interest such as:
   a. Performing operating assignments?
   b. Writing or approving department procedures?
   c. Designing information or internal control systems?

10. Do formal and informal reporting relationships with the internal audit department have the potential to create conflicts of interest? Describe those reporting relationships and potential conflicts of interest.

8

TAX

The scope and the responsibility of tax services in organizations vary by tax reporting and record-keeping requirements, and by the technical depth and organizational structure of the tax group. Most organizations cannot cost-effectively meet their tax requirements without a responsible, permanent group. An effectively organized and experienced tax group can contribute significantly to financial function effectiveness and, more importantly, to the overall profitability of an organization. Major ongoing contributions of the tax group include:

- Optimizing the effective tax rate
- Preparing all tax returns and administering compliance
- Ensuring integrity between book and tax records
- Advising the organization to maximize tax benefits arising from current and future operations

- Developing a corporate tax policy for all items of taxes and for all aspects of company operations

Tax reporting relationships are shaped by the size of the tax group, scope of responsibilities, and staff experience. The tax group may report to the controller, treasurer, general counsel, or chief financial officer. An effectiveness review of the tax function should consider:

- Tax environment
- Tax policy, procedure, and compliance
- Tax planning

The scope of the effectiveness review will vary by organization, based on the level of support for major tax activities routinely obtained from outside tax specialists. Other considerations, such as the existence of foreign operations, also will shape the responsibilities and the scope of the effectiveness review.

TAX ENVIRONMENT

The tax environment defines the scope and level of activity of the overall tax function. Evaluating the tax environment considers the tax requirements of the organization as well as the technical capabilities and organizational structure of the permanent tax group. Understanding the tax environment includes recognizing the role of outside specialists to meet tax requirements. Evaluating the environment also should reveal whether tax goals and opportunities are achieved effectively. The objectives of evaluating the tax environment include determining:

- Qualitative and quantitative goals of tax and how those goals are measured

- Mix of centralized and decentralized activity
- Relationships between tax and other organizational units
- Tax-functional responsibilities
- Extent of tax documentation
- Use of computer-based systems to support tax activities
- Completeness and appropriateness of tax compliance matters
- Level of tax-planning initiatives and responsiveness

Defining the tax environment establishes boundaries for performing an effectiveness review. Understanding tax goals and how they are measured should establish the basis to judge whether tax activities are appropriate, consistent with the organization's overall objectives, and achieved effectively. Management needs to know that the mix of centralized and decentralized tax activities is appropriate for the tax services required by the organization. Defining the relationships between tax and other organizational units should detect gaps between management's perception and the reality of tax's contribution to the organization. It also should indicate the degree of management support of tax goals and responsibilities. Tax documentation should delineate the structure and controls of the tax function. Reliance on computer-based systems may indicate the complexity and sophistication of available tax services.

TAX ENVIRONMENT ATTRIBUTES

1. Define corporate tax goals and objectives. What are the:
   a. Qualitative goals?
   b. Quantitative goals?
2. What measures and criteria are used to evaluate tax services?

3. Determine the extent of and reasons for centralized and decentralized activity for:
   a. Federal tax compliance
   b. International tax compliance
   c. State and other tax compliance
   d. Payroll, pension, and benefits compliance
   e. Tax planning

4. What are the scope and level of relationships between tax and other organizational units including:
   a. Controlling?
   b. Chief financial officer?
   c. Treasury?
   d. Internal audit?
   e. General counsel?

   Are these direct report relationships or informal relationships? Does the tax group participate in advising line management, parent or holding companies, and so forth, regarding tax activity and requirements?

5. Determine whether tax responsibilities for federal tax compliance include:
   a. Calculations of tax provisions and analysis of effective tax rates?
   b. Analysis of current and deferred liability accounts provision, including cushion analysis?
   c. Reviews of key ledger accounts and consolidating entries impacting tax liability?
   d. Cost of goods sold and inventories?
   e. Preparation of consolidated and separate returns?
   f. Schedule M-1 and Schedule M-2 reconciliation?
   g. Estimated federal income tax payments?
   h. Monitoring of compliance for domestic joint ventures?
   i. Research and development tax credits?
   j. Fixed asset tax control reviews?

    k. Revenue agent examinations?

    l. Dividend, interest, and miscellaneous income reports (Form 1099)?

6. Identify responsibility for federal tax compliance by permanent tax group, other functional departments, and outside tax specialists.

7. Identify responsibilities for international tax compliance by a permanent tax group, other functional departments, or outside tax specialists for:
   a. DISC and FSC reporting
   b. Foreign corporations
   c. U.S. and foreign sales and expense reviews
   d. Subsidiary or branch foreign returns
   e. Joint venture, partnership, and noncontrolled foreign corporation compliance
   f. Foreign tax credit and gross-up
   g. Revenue agent examination
   h. Boycott reporting
   i. U.S. companies controlled by foreign shareholders (Form 5472)

8. Identify responsibilities for state and other tax compliance performed by a permanent tax group, other functional departments, or outside tax specialists for:
   a. State return preparation and extensions
   b. State apportionment data
   c. State license, franchise, property tax, and so forth
   d. Sales and use tax
   e. Excise and severance tax
   f. Personal property tax
   g. Real property tax
   h. Revenue agent examination coordination
   i. Unitary taxation

9. Identify responsibilities for payroll, benefits, and pension compliance performed by a permanent tax group, other functional departments, or outside tax specialists for:
   a. Federal unemployment tax (FUTA), FICA, and federal withholding deposits and forms
   b. State and local payroll tax reporting
   c. Additional compensation reporting
   d. Unemployment filings and data
   e. Forms W-2 and W-4
   f. WIN and jobs tax credits
   g. Employee benefits compliance with ERISA and tax rules
   h. Expatriate tax advice

10. Identify responsibilities for federal and state tax planning performed by a permanent tax group, other functional departments, or outside tax specialists for:
    a. Effective tax rates (techniques, legal entity impact, alternatives)
    b. Liquidations and reorganizations
    c. Mergers, acquisitions, and buyouts
    d. Tax review of significant agreements
    e. Review of new regulations, statutes, case law, private letter rulings
    f. Multistate tax planning
    g. Unitary taxation

11. Identify responsibilities for international tax planning performed by a permanent tax group, other functional departments, or outside tax specialists for:
    a. Long-range planning
    b. Foreign tax monitoring
    c. Foreign tax credit and dividend planning
    d. Controlled foreign corporation activity
    e. Review of operations for tax benefits from intercompany pricing, cost allocations, and export sales

   f. Allocation of expenses to sources of income

   g. Repatriation of foreign cash and earnings

   h. Tax implications of foreign currency management

   i. Review of new regulations, statutes, case law, private letter rulings

12. Identify responsibilities for payroll, pension, and benefits planning performed by a permanent tax group, other functional departments, or outside tax specialists for:

   a. Tax-qualified benefit plans

   b. Tax nonqualified benefit plans

   c. Expatriates

13. Are job descriptions current and complete for activities performed by the permanent tax group?

14. Are tax procedures documented? Do they accurately document the scope of tax activities?

15. Identify key tax policy issues. Are tax activities consistent with current tax policies?

16. Is the permanent tax group able to meet specific tax objectives given its organizational and staffing charts including identification of peak workload periods? Consider overtime levels and work backlogs.

17. Is the tax staff qualified to effectively achieve tax objectives? Consider whether:

   a. Education, technical, and experience backgrounds of tax personnel are adequate to tax services required by the organization

   b. Tax personnel have sufficient technical knowledge and computer "literacy" for available tax systems and applications

   c. Tax personnel maintain or increase their professional skills through activities such as courses and seminars

18. If outside tax specialists are used to meet tax needs, identify reasons for using these services, including lack of available internal resources, specialized skills, and so on.

19. Evaluate the benefits and weaknesses of all major internal and external tax reference and preparation systems.

20. Is general ledger integration adequate for accessing tax impact accounts at the legal entity and organization levels?

21. Evaluate the specific controls over transaction flow from subsystems to the general ledger that impact tax records and compliance reporting, such as payroll.

22. Do data collection methods and information systems facilitate accumulating financial information for tax compliance and planning?

23. To what extent and effectiveness are computer-based systems, including microcomputers, used for tax services?

TAX POLICY, PROCEDURE, AND COMPLIANCE

Tax policy provides the broad framework that defines tax responsibilities, information needs, and the approach to meet tax planning and compliance needs. Policy directly influences the attitudes of personnel involved in tax functions. It defines tax priorities and necessary qualifications to meet requirements.

Tax procedures ensure consistent performance of activities to achieve planning and compliance requirements. Clearly defined and well-documented procedures provide an effective comparison of actual against recommended conduct of tax activities. Failure to follow established procedures may reduce tax effectiveness and produce problems that include failure to realize full tax benefits, optimize tax rates, and comply with regulatory requirements.

Organizations comply with tax requirements by accurate and timely preparation of returns and reports based upon tax-related accounts. Compliance includes ensuring that requirements for tax-related transactions are met. It also should include analysis of accounts into which these transactions flow. Tax compliance dictates that managerial and operational activities conform to relevant statutes and regulations of federal, state, local, and foreign taxing authorities.

The objectives of evaluating tax policy, procedure, and compliance in support of tax responsibility include determining the completeness and scope of:

- Corporate tax policy statements and procedures
- Federal, state, local, and other tax compliance
- International tax compliance
- Payroll, pension, and benefits tax compliance

Effectively performed tax compliance activities should avoid tax penalties, improve tax planning, manage tax liability, and optimize the corporate effective tax rate.

TAX POLICY, PROCEDURE, AND COMPLIANCE ATTRIBUTES

1. Identify tax policies approved by top management.
2. To what extent does tax policy address compliance with domestic and foreign laws?
3. Does tax policy specify responsibilities for tax compliance?
4. Do tax procedures effectively integrate tax goals, objectives, and activities into overall corporate plans? Do procedures:
   a. Define tax input to management activities and include

the impact of management activities on tax-planning objectives?

  b. Define tax involvement in documentation reviews of agreements, mergers, and so forth?
  c. Identify tax participation in development of company-wide financial systems?

5. Do tax procedures define responsibilities of tax and other financial personnel for availability, quality, and timing of required tax function for tax compliance and planning?
  a. Include periodic review of general ledger accounts to ensure proper tax treatment?
  b. Reflect low materiality limits consistent with tax compliance requirements?
  c. Include reconciliation of companywide account totals from management reporting to legal entity formats?
  d. Define responsibilities for producing accurate tax-related data and for responding to outside audit requirements?

6. Do procedures and controls enable the tax department to monitor any tax activities outside the department's direct control?

7. Do tax administrative procedures provide:
  a. Training plans to maintain competence of the tax staff?
  b. Periodic review of tax software to increase the effectiveness of tax services?
  c. Steps to update current tax procedures?

8. What returns are filed for each of the following tax authorities:
  a. Federal?
  b. State and local?
  c. Foreign?
  d. Payroll, pension, and benefits?

9. Evaluate the adequacy of supporting documentation maintained for all tax filings.

10. Does the company have recurring problems with late filings of returns, assessed penalties, or late payment of taxes?

11. Have audits performed by any taxing authorities resulted in significant adjustments?

12. Is adequate documentation maintained on settling issues raised by taxing authorities?

13. Do estimated taxes paid routinely exceed taxes payable?

14. Are federal income tax estimates and payments prepared in a timely manner?

TAX PLANNING

Tax planning plays an important role in the financial function's contribution to profit. Tax planning must be integrated in daily operations and in merger, acquisition, and reorganization plans and strategy. For example, the timing of dividend payments and the availability and use of tax credits can affect business planning decisions. Tax planning also can impact pension and benefit planning by preventing improper installation of employee benefit plans to avoid the loss of tax benefits to the corporation and employees.

The objectives of reviewing the tax-planning function include determining that:

- Foreign operations tax liabilities and tax effects are properly integrated into overall corporate plans
- Effective tax rates affected by tax deferral, reduction techniques, legal entity tax provision, and alternative tax strategies are properly analyzed and monitored
- Infrequent events such as reorganizations, mergers, and acquisitions are reviewed by tax planning in a timely manner

195

- Payroll, pension, and benefits programs are reviewed for potential tax treatment and for recommendations to make further improvements

Tax planning often requires models and access to financial data to support analysis of alternatives. Tax planning also should have access to business plans to understand the organization's strategy and direction. Successful tax planning depends on the level and timing of tax department interaction with management to provide input to the corporate planning process.

TAX PLANNING ATTRIBUTES

1. Are tax deferral and reduction techniques adequate to optimize the organization's effective tax rate?
2. Are reviews of legal entity tax provisions and liabilities used to identify opportunities to improve operating results?
3. Are tax strategies periodically reviewed using alternative operating scenarios and conditions?
4. Does tax planning consider the effects of corporate reorganizations with respect to:
   a. Tax strategy?
   b. Close-down reserves and start-up costs under various reorganization scenarios?
   c. Tax impact of pending reorganizations?
5. Does tax planning include analyses of the tax impacts of proposed mergers, acquisitions, and buyouts?
6. Does tax planning include monitoring merger, acquisition, and buyout activities to prevent tax problems and to meet reporting requirements?
7. Are transaction reviews conducted to determine tax impacts

of proposed agreements, such as joint ventures, licenses, and royalty?

8. Does tax planning prepare analyses of the impacts of new statutes and regulations?

9. Are controlled foreign corporations structured to optimize tax benefits?

10. For foreign subsidiaries, evaluate the appropriateness and extent of integrating tax accrual and liability into overall corporate plans.

11. Evaluate the effect of foreign accumulated earnings and profits for dividend payout and tax effects, including use of tax credits on federal returns.

12. Are international operations structured to optimize tax benefits from practices such as intercompany pricing and cost allocations?

13. Do tax personnel based in the United States participate in foreign tax planning and compliance activities, including examinations by foreign tax authorities?

14. Together with the human resource function, does tax planning adequately participate in developing and improving employee benefit programs to ensure optimum tax treatment for the organization and employee?

15. Together with the human resource function, does tax planning communicate compensation and reimbursement programs to expatriates to minimize U.S. and foreign tax costs?